Praise for *Worth Every Penny*

"Sarah Petty has rocked the photography industry and put big money in many photographers' pockets with her boutique business model. This book is the real deal and can help any small business owner who wants to make money doing what they love."

—George Varanakis, executive vice president and group publisher of Wedding & Portrait Photographers International

"This book shows you how to make better and more profitable sales in your business, growing by increasing your value offering and making your customers happier."

—Brian Tracy, author of *The Psychology of Selling*

"I honestly have to say that *Worth Every Penny* is one of the best business books I've ever read. The information is presented clearly, in an easy-to-digest format. The stories are delightful and memorable, and perfectly illustrate the important teaching points. This book is a combination of solid marketing and business advice, presented in a fresh new way, and some engaging twists that had me taking notes for my business and my clients. Bravo!"

—Pamela Bruner, author of *Tapping into Ultimate Success*

"Their line 'boutique is a business model—not a gift shop' says much. I knew Sarah and Erin were wickedly smart about this the first time I met them. Sarah built one of the most profitable photography businesses in the country at rocket-speed. They both come at this from experience, not theory. Their terrific book, *Worth Every Penny*, offers a million dollars worth of good sense about building businesses that have unique positioning, thrill customers, and need not default to discounting."

—Dan S. Kennedy, author, *No B.S. Price Strategy* (with Jason Marrs), *No B.S. Wealth Attraction in the New Economy*, and 21 other business books; marketing strategist and consultant, and multi-millionaire serial entrepreneur; www.NoBSBooks.com, www.DanKennedy.com

WORTH

EVERY

PENNY

WORTH

BUILD A BUSINESS THAT THRILLS YOUR CUSTOMERS

EVERY

and STILL CHARGE WHAT YOU'RE WORTH

PENNY

SARAH PETTY ✤ ERIN VERBECK

GREENLEAF
BOOK GROUP PRESS

Published by Greenleaf Book Group Press
Austin, Texas
www.gbgpress.com

Distributed by Greenleaf Book Group LLC

For ordering information or special discounts for bulk purchases, please contact Greenleaf Book Group LLC at PO Box 91869, Austin, TX 78709, 512.891.6100.

Design and composition by Greenleaf Book Group LLC
Cover design by Greenleaf Book Group LLC
Author photos by Sarah Petty Photography

Publisher's Cataloging-In-Publication Data
(Prepared by The Donohue Group, Inc.)
Petty, Sarah.
   Worth every penny : how to charge what you're worth when everyone else is discounting / Sarah Petty [and] Erin Verbeck. — 1st ed.
      p. ; cm.
   Includes bibliographical references.
   ISBN: 978-1-60832-277-0
   1. New business enterprises—Planning. 2. Pricing. 3. Small business marketing.
4. Success in business. I. Verbeck, Erin. II. Title.
HD62.5 .P48 2012
658.1/1   2011945096

Part of the Tree Neutral® program, which offsets the number of trees consumed in the production and printing of this book by taking proactive steps, such as planting trees in direct proportion to the number of trees used: www.treeneutral.com

Printed in the United States of America on acid-free paper

TreeNeutral®

12 13 14 15 16   10 9 8 7 6 5 4 3 2 1

First Edition

To my parents, Joel and Pam Tjelmeland.
The entrepreneur and the creative.
You're my inspiration. I love you.
—Sarah

To my husband, Chris Verbeck.
You're the cheese to my macaroni.
I love you.
—Erin

And to the many clients of Sarah Petty Photography
and The Joy of Marketing. Thank you all for allowing us
to pursue our passions every single day.

CONTENTS

Foreword xi

Start Here 1

{THE BASICS}
**BOUTIQUE IS A BUSINESS MODEL,
NOT A GIFT SHOP** 7

{SECTION I}
BRANDING 15

   1: Why Boutique Businesses Have to Get Branding Right . 17

   2: Boutique Brand Essentials 25

   3: To Rebrand or Not to Rebrand? 39

{SECTION II}
**PRODUCTS, SERVICES,
AND THE CUSTOMER EXPERIENCE** 45

   4: Making Boutique Products and Services Worth More ... 47

   5: The High-Touch Experience 55

   6: Building a Team That Completes the
       Boutique Experience 65

   7: When the Boutique Experience Goes Wrong 71

{SECTION III}

PRICE 79

8: Price Isn't Everything 81

9: The Boutique Pricing Strategy 87

10: The Scars of the Sale 97

{SECTION IV}

MARKETING & SELLING 111

11: The Boutique Marketing Difference 113

12: Building Your Database and Marketing Your Business .. 121

13: The Lowdown on Low-Touch Advertising Options 139

14: Nurturing and Rewarding Your Best Clients 147

15: How to Sell Boutique 163

16: Rules to Live By as a Boutique Business Owner 173

Conclusion: You CAN Be Worth Every Penny 179

Epilogue: For Those Who Haven't Done It Yet 183

Acknowledgments 189

Additional Resources 193

FOREWORD

I'VE WRITTEN A FEW FOREWORDS in my life, but only for special books. Books that touched upon an entrepreneurial subject that had long ago been beaten to death but that did so with a verve, style, and substance that illuminated the well worn, weary subject in a way that stimulated a new and original take on it.

Of course, in my mind, this book is such a book.

How to create a different company, a company that takes the ordinary and delivers it as the extraordinary?

A company like so many examples in this book.

A hot dog stand that isn't just a hot dog stand.

A photography business that isn't just a photography business.

In short, these are companies much like the greatest companies ever created—like Apple, like Zappos, like Starbucks, and like (I wish) so many more—but they are also companies you've probably never heard of. The owners of these companies learned and put into practice the fine art of turning a raw commodity into a blazingly original product.

And after all, that's the point of this book—to demonstrate to you the innumerable ways in which you can make your company worth every penny, and even more.

So, to get a shot of entrepreneurial derring-do, and to take a true picture of what your company is doing (or could be doing), sit down, put your feet up, rest your weary soul, and read, read, read. You're about to go on an unexpectedly exciting journey. I know, because I did. And I loved every second of it.

Michael E. Gerber
Author of the E-Myth books
Founder, Origination
Founder and Chief Dreamer, The Dreaming Room

START HERE

STARTING A BUSINESS IS SCARY. You've taken the leap, quit your full-time job, and decided to follow your passion. It was thrilling at first, and it felt so great to get out of that cubicle. But business didn't take off quite as quickly as you'd hoped. You don't have as many clients as you planned for. Sales are slow. And now you need cash, quickly, unless you want to sell your car and start eating ramen noodles every night. So you offered a 50-percent off sale and spread the news to everyone you could think of. You ran an ad in the newspaper. You sent emails to your entire database. You told the world on Facebook and Twitter. You're handing out coupons like there's no tomorrow.

Stop.

You're trying to fix the wrong problem.

That approach won't do you any good. In fact, it can do incalculable damage to your brand, your profit margins, and the long-term value of your business. There's a better way to do business. And that's why we're writing this book.

For the portrait photographer who believes that her prices need to mirror the portrait pricing at Sears, there's a better way to compete. For the graphic designer who thinks he will only get enough business if he charges the lowest hourly rate, there's a better way to compete. For the restaurateur who's tried and failed at every type of advertising, there's a better way to compete. And for any small business whose phone isn't ringing, who can't get customers in the door, there's a better way to compete. Anyone in a specialty business can benefit from this book.

Erin and I learned the lessons in this book from experience. In the summer of 2000, I was pregnant with twins. I decided to give up my long days at an amazingly creative advertising agency, HIP Advertising. It was a job I had spent my whole career working toward (this is where Erin and I first met). But I knew that it was time to focus on my family, turn my longtime hobby into a real business, and open my first photography studio. After my twins were born, I invested in a professionally designed logo and spent the summer painting and fixing up a studio space. I was having a blast—I was full of the excitement and anticipation of starting my own business. Two weeks before the 9/11 attacks, Sarah Petty Photography officially opened its doors. I'd been open barely long enough to get a credit card in my business name when, overnight, the marketplace was overwhelmed with anxiety. People were scared, and our economy screeched to a halt.

Yes, Sarah Petty Photography opened its doors two weeks before a world-changing catastrophe and major economic crisis. But by viewing marketing through a different lens, my business was able to grow quickly and profitably.

Fast-forward to today. There's still fear about the economy. There's still anxiety. There's still hesitation. And, among business owners, there's still a widespread assumption that every transaction is driven by price, that discounting is the only way to compete in the marketplace, and that quantity of business outweighs quality of business. We are here to disagree with that assumption. We're here to reveal a different perspective, a model that can work better for your small business. The Joy of Marketing was formed so we could teach small business owners how to implement the boutique business model that has produced industry-leading profits in my photography business and has allowed me to have the family life I desired. As both companies grew, it was increasingly difficult for me to keep them both profitable and maintain my family balance. It was time for Erin. After leaving the advertising agency, Erin and I had taken separate paths, both earning our MBAs, both having worked for some of the top brands in the world. We had often dreamed about working together again and it was time. Once we joined forces, we knew that there were a lot of small business owners in the world we could help.

This small-business book is simple. You'll learn how to create a decision-making filter so you can do what you love and charge what you're worth. Inside these pages, you won't find corporate jargon. There's no deep theory like the kind you'd find in a marketing textbook or college class. Instead you'll find simple, straightforward ideas and easy-to-implement action steps, written in everyday language by people who are doing it every day, that will consistently deliver results. You'll find examples from business owners—people all over the world who live and breathe their businesses every day. And you'll discover a new perspective—a fresh way of filtering all that you do, all that you sell, and how you price yourself for profit.

This book is for people who want to pursue their life dream by making a business out their passion. It's for people who own a small business and might be feeling the pressure to discount in order to stay alive. It's for people who want to own a small business but don't know where to start. And it's also for business owners who already "get it" but feel that something is missing. You're working all the time and don't have time to think about being profitable. You may already sell "boutique" products, items, and services that are customized, hard to find, and nearly impossible to replicate, but you may not understand how to market them in way that enables you to charge more. Maybe you own a small business that offers a fantastically over-the-top customer experience but aren't finding the clients who are willing to pay more for it. This book lays out an alternative business model that will help you work less, bring in more profit, have more time to be creative, and attract clients who appreciate what you do and are willing to pay for it.

To start off, we'll show you a business model that frees you from needless price wars and gives you the boutique edge. With the boutique business model, you won't have to work all the time. You won't worry about out-discounting your competitors. Once you have the boutique mind-set, you'll start building a customer base that loves you, comes back to you again and again, and tells their friends about you.

The four core areas of this book are:

1. Branding: We'll show you why branding is crucial for boutique businesses. Whether you're building a brand from scratch or refining your current one, we'll show you how to manage, strengthen, and communicate your brand in every aspect of your business so that your marketing attracts the right buyers.

2. Products, Services, and Customer Experience: To succeed as a boutique business, you can't be vanilla in anything you do. Your offerings need to be more specialized or custom than what the discounters are offering. And we'll show you how you can create experiences that give you an insanely loyal customer base.

3. Price: Are you tired of trying to compete with the discounters? As a boutique business owner, you will see that you don't have to. Learn how to price for profit and how knee-jerk discounts in an attempt to attract new customers will hurt your business. We show you alternatives to discounting that will still excite and reward your best clients without devaluing your brand.

4. Marketing and Sales: Boutique businesses don't have the budget to market like big corporations. We'll show you that you have the upper hand: with your limited scope and healthy margins, you've got the power to nurture relationships and get creative with your database, generating you far better results than plastering ads in the paper or buying a TV spot.

Throughout this book, you'll also hear from other successful boutique business owners as they share their real-world stories and insights. You'll find practical action steps that you can implement today. You'll get loads of perspective on how to make your offerings worth every penny of your premium profitable price.

In this book, we're bringing to the table the knowledge that we've gained by working at some of the world's largest brands, by spending years in ad agencies, and by succeeding in our own small businesses. We don't just get it; we're doing it. We want you to be able to build the world you dreamed of, where you have the freedom to pursue your passion and make a profit.

THE BASICS

Boutique Is a Business Model, Not a Gift Shop

WHAT DOES BOUTIQUE MEAN?

It's a fancy little word. But just wait until you see what it can do for your business.

A cosmetic dentist in Spokane, a flower shop owner in Richmond, a luxury real estate broker in the Hamptons, a self-employed portrait photographer in Minneapolis—they're all boutique business owners. *Being a boutique business isn't about what you sell.* It's not about your geographic location, your storefront, or even the size of your business. Instead, "being boutique" is about how you operate—it's a model of doing business, a filter for your business decisions, and a mind-set that makes your customers say you were worth every penny.

When you're boutique, your products or services are specialized and customized. They're cooler. They're more fabulous. They're more personalized. They're more valuable. And they're almost impossible to imitate, because they're based on your personality and talents.

When you're boutique, the service you give to customers is more personal. You know the special ways your clients like to be treated, their habits, their lifestyles, and their desires. And because your margins aren't so tight, you can afford to go the extra mile for them.

When you're boutique, the way you approach business is different, the way you approach branding, marketing, and advertising is different. Your business rules are different. Your price structure is different. And the way you compete in the marketplace is different.

Let's talk about what you're not. As a boutique, you're the opposite of a big-box store. You're not open all the time or on every corner. You're not trying to get as many customers as possible; you're trying to get as many "right" customers as possible—customers who want to buy your products and services from you, at your price, because you are providing them something they can't get anywhere else. And, because you don't have the buying power that the big brands do, you shouldn't try to compete on price.

> "'Being boutique' is about how you operate—it's a model of doing business, a filter for your business decisions, and a mindset that makes your customers say you were worth every penny."

The same is true for any lower-priced business that is a competitor. Whether it's a stay-at-home mom offering professional photography on the cheap or a new chain business that is undercutting your prices, you're not truly in competition just because they sell a product or service similar to yours.

Instead, you can beat your competition by catering to the niches, not to the masses.

Maybe you own a bike shop, and Walmart decides to carry the same line of bikes that makes up a significant percentage of your sales. As a boutique business, you shouldn't panic. Because you're a competitive cyclist, and you take the time to learn how your customers ride. You recommend trails that match your customers' abilities, accessories to improve their performance, and seats and handlebars to best fit their body types. Walmart can't offer that.

Or perhaps you're the nail salon owner who sought out a special line of nail polish when Maggie, one of your regulars, developed an allergy to the polish you use. You could be anyone—mortgage broker, sandwich shop owner, tax consultant, barista—who views customers as flesh-and-blood people rather than as units of sale.

Because you operate within the boutique business model, you're positioned away from the pack. You're just as rare as an original piece of art. We want you to relish the fact that you're one of a kind, and then start charging more for it. And that's what we're here to do.

Businesses that compete on price can't invade your territory. When you're a boutique business, you're the expert, you're the personal consultant, you're the teacher, you're the person looking to thrill your customers every single time.

THE BOUTIQUE ADVANTAGE

When you embrace this business model, you have the "boutique advantage." As you read through this book, you'll not only discover the rewards, freedom, and gratification that come with using the boutique business model; you'll also discover through many stories and case studies how being boutique gives you a sustainable competitive advantage—leaving the big-box stores and other discounters trying to follow in your footsteps. You can never sustain price as an advantage. Walmart, Jiffy Lube, Lowe's, Toys "R" Us, PetSmart, Kohl's, JCPenney, and Dunkin' Donuts cast the big nets. They offer products that appeal to the masses. But they leave a lot of holes to fill. Who carries all of the other more specialized products they pass over? Who builds the customer relationships these corporations don't have time to build? Who offers a mind-blowing experience? You do. And that's a powerful advantage. But don't fret if you're not there yet. It's more than just slapping higher prices on your offerings. We wrote this book to teach you how to get there.

You have the boutique advantage because you don't have to compete by offering discounts. Your higher profit margins and strong relationships with your clients allow you to invest in inimitable products and spend time providing a deeper level of service and expertise—all because you don't have to match your competitors' weekly sales.

Because you don't have to work 24/7 to make payroll, you can travel and invest in the latest education and bring it back to your clients. The fact that you have the time to educate and pamper each individual client is an advantage over your discounting competitors.

Do you think it's impossible that you actually have the advantage over the discounting kings?

Consider that in order to attract the volume they need to show a profit, the big brands must constantly discount their products or services. To maintain low prices, they often pressure manufacturers to simplify their specs so they can be sold cheaper. They focus on deriving profits from selling volume—a million big-brand polyester baby booties instead of just twenty-five made of the most exquisite 100 percent all-natural Egyptian cotton with gorgeous hand embroidery. You, on the other hand, can offer better products—products that show your passion.

Many big-brand retailers are now attempting to provide more personalized customer service and more unique products. From personal shopping services and private sales to credit card holders, they are trying to compete with boutique businesses. But they'll never be able to truly compete with you. Sure, they can distribute these products and services on a mass scale, but their margins are so tight due to discounts that even their "specialized" products soon become commodities. They'll never have the time or margins that enable you to make your products stand out in the market. And, they'll never be able to have the relationships that you have with your customers.

Your advantage as a boutique business should become clearer with every page of this book.

THE BOUTIQUE FILTER: "AM I APPROACHING MY BUSINESS AS A BOUTIQUE BUSINESS?"

Boutique: it's not a gift shop. It's the filter through which all decisions are made. It's the products you sell. It's the way you treat customers. It's the way you educate customers, because you're an expert. It's how you manage your client and vendor relationships. It's what helps you decide how to market and promote your business. And it's what helps you manage the growth of your business.

How does all this boutique bliss happen? It's not when you become more crafty, or artsy, or creative, or sell fancy doilies or high-end stationery. Instead, it happens with a simple shift in your mind-set. It happens when you stop seeing "boutique" as "gift shop" and start seeing it as a business and marketing model that can help you charge what you're worth. It starts when you take a boutique approach to branding. It starts when you take a boutique approach to your product mix and pricing strategy, your customer service philosophy, and the experience you offer your clients. It starts with a boutique approach to marketing, advertising, networking, and promotion.

Keep in mind that you'll need to customize your boutique filter—what works for one boutique business may not work for you. You'll need to learn how to operate not as just any boutique but as *your* boutique. As you read through the chapters of this book, you'll discover some ideas that work wonders for your business right out of the box, some that need to be tweaked to fit your business, and others that may not fit your business at all. That's okay. We challenge you to keep an open mind and use each new idea as an opportunity to develop your boutique filter.

To get started, let's apply the boutique filter to branding.

BRANDING

Without a remarkable brand, a boutique business is nothing. That might seem a little dramatic, but it's true. If people don't know what you're about, if your business looks different every time they see you, if they can't rely on you for a spectacular, one-of-a-kind experience every time, what's to stop them from going next door for the cheaper products of your competitors? Your brand is how people feel about you. To charge what you're worth, it's essential to carefully craft and manage your reputation for being the best at what you do before you start marketing. Your brand lays the foundation for attracting the right clients and increasing the results of your marketing efforts. Your fantastic, reliable brand will put you ahead of the competition, whether the competition looks like a huge corporation or the brand-challenged mom-and-pop next door, and justify the premium prices that make yours a healthy boutique business.

CHAPTER 1

Why Boutique Businesses Have to Get Branding Right

YOUR BRAND IS IMPORTANT.

That's an understatement.

Years ago, you could go to your corner grocer and ask for flour. The grocer would scoop it out of a big bin for you and put it into a paper bag. There were no brands to choose from. There was no differentiation even between different types of flour. Products were commodities.

Once brands were introduced, the world changed. Now you have a choice on what type of flour you want. One brand is made locally, from farmers you know and trust. Yet another brand donates a percentage of its profits to a charitable cause you support. And yet another brand uses pesticide-free wheat. Now you can have a product that means something to you, and you are willing to pay more for it because of the brand. The brand now stands for something more than just the flour in the bag. As a consumer, you have choices.

Being a boutique business, your brand is fundamental for your survival. It's critical to charging what you're worth, because as you'll learn later in the book, you're going to be charging more. If you want to stop discounting, you must build a strong brand. Without it, you might as well start dropping your prices today. A disjointed brand attracts price-sensitive buyers. Like sharks circling wounded prey, cheap consumers can sense a brand that is limping along and will push for lower prices. As soon as you start making decisions based on the wrong consumer, your perspective as a business owner gets skewed. And that's when you feel the mounting pressure to discount.

WHAT IS A BRAND?

Branding is a smudgy term that changes depending on who you ask for a definition. Think of it this way. Imagine one client, friend, relative, or neighbor who thinks you are the absolute bomb at what you do—they think you are the smartest, or most talented, or most creative, or most gifted person in your craft. (As a rule of thumb, you must exclude your mother from your list, simply because all mothers think their kids are the bomb. And, let's be honest: mothers applaud when their children poop.) Okay, got that fan in mind? Can you envision how he or she perceives you? It's that person's perception of you—the way you shine in his or her mind—that you want to expose to everyone who could be an ideal client. This is your brand. It's how people feel about you. It is the feelings conjured up when someone mentions your name or that of your business. It's like a dog whistle; it signals to your ideal client that you are just right for them.

Monster companies, like Apple, Budweiser, Coca-Cola, and FedEx, have very deep brands. Their brands are seen, felt, touched, and heard all over the world. And, although you may not believe that you have to pay as much attention to your boutique brand as these companies do, we beg to differ.

Being boutique, your brand has to be more dialed in than the brands of the big-box stores, because one mistake can leave you unrecognizable. It is easy for the gigantic companies to overcome one misstep—they have zillions of impressions in the marketplace. One misstep (alienating their core customer base in a marketing piece) is a drop in a very large bucket. Big brands have the resources to shout from the mountaintops.

But we only have a little megaphone that can't be heard past the end of the block. That's why we have to make sure we get it right. We have a smaller budget, limited reach, and lower frequency, so when we make a branding mistake, it can cause a lot of harm. The stakes are higher for us because we are smaller. Every misstep is a big splash in your small pond.

BECOMING A BRAND

When I first started charging for my passion of photography I, like many of you, didn't understand how to charge for something that I loved to do anyway. I was guessing at pricing, charging my photography clients $75 for thirty-six hand-printed black-and-white proofs. Between the cost of film, processing, and printing, I was barely breaking even if the client didn't place an additional order. I was banking on the fact that people would love my photography and order more. After I had two clients in a row come to me thrilled about my work and gushing about what I did and then *not* place an order, I was frustrated. I learned from talking to my happy clients that I was earning the reputation of being a fantastic value—people could invest a little and get a lot. Then, two weeks before I went full time and opened my studio, I attended my first Professional Photographers of America convention. I learned about cost of sales, pricing, and how to sell. I realized that, because I was underpriced, people were not seeing me as a brand worth paying more for; to them, I was just a photographer. To get the prices I wanted, I needed to create a brand that would justify the profitable prices I wanted to charge.

I knew I didn't want to be a commodity, so I quickly refocused. I continued to insist that I would *not* diminish my passion and dedication to perfection by ever sending out a coupon. I decided to create a dynamic promotional piece to showcase my style, my work, and my love for photography. This piece had to communicate my passion for what I do so that I could attract the right consumers—ones who loved what I did and weren't lured in by a cheap price. Nobody in my market specialized in the whimsical, playful style that I had created to photograph babies and toddlers. These were the things that had to be communicated in my promotional piece. Hard-selling my services wouldn't have connected with the customers I wanted to attract on an emotional level. The people who loved the images in that promotional piece wouldn't care about price. They would connect because I had tapped into an emotion or desire.

You can check out this promotional piece at www.worth everypennybook.com/promotionalpiece. It opened four times. Each flap had minimal copy but oodles of emotion, making a deep connection with the prospect. And, instead of telling the world that I was a great photographer through cumbersome self-promotional wording, I showed them that I would dump all of my energy into creating something magical for them to hang in their homes, giving them warm-fuzzy feelings for years to come. The promotional piece made a massive impact upon receipt by parents of new babies. The first week I mailed it, a new client came in and ordered twice as much as my previous largest order. A steady stream of new clients followed.

The right clients were calling consistently, and I was showing steady growth. Referrals were starting to come in as well. However, it was hard to measure the impact my efforts were having on my brand. How long would it be before people would look at my work and immediately know that I had become more than simply a photographer?

Fewer than six months after mailing that first promotional piece, my husband and I listed our own house for sale. During an open house, a young woman, toddler in hand, stroller in front, and huge diaper bag on arm, walked through the front door, pointed at the portrait on the wall, and blurted, "Is that a Sarah Petty!?"

She was excited. She had recognized my work immediately. My brand meant something to her.

My initial response to her spirited excitement was embarrassment. I was speechless. I was seconds away from a reaction, but had no idea what it would be—laughter, hysterical sobbing, puking? This young woman was, by all definitions, my ideal client. And she was thrilled to see my work.

That was the day I realized that my brand had meaning to at least one person. And it reinforced my belief that building a strong brand would continue to help me attract clients who were willing to invest more so that I could continue to create the time-intensive, magical experience and powerful images that would blow them away.

YOU NEED A STRONG BRAND TO CHARGE WHAT YOU'RE WORTH

Being a boutique business, your brand needs to be stronger. You have the opportunity to make people fall in love with your brand, thanks to the enthusiasm, personal flair, and individual attention you present to each of your clients. Even with your limited resources, you can beat big companies at the branding game because these power-players will never be able to offer something to their clients that you can offer—you. You are an integral part of your brand—the one that's built on your passion. You carry the brunt of the load. Your distribution might be slower than a big-box competitor, your marketing budget might be restricted, but your prices shouldn't even be in the same ballpark as the big-box stores. When your brand exposes you and your talents, customers will choose your company over and over and over again.

Sue Thompson, owner of The Sue Thompson Gallery, in Springfield, Illinois, got a firsthand demonstration of how highly people in her community value her brand. She offers art, handcrafted jewelry, and other one-of-a-kind items. And she's built a strong brand—so strong that her hand-painted, store-branded bags are coveted. A customer asked Sue to exchange a gift she had received from a friend. Happy to oblige, Sue opened the store-branded bag to find a product she had never carried. The gift-giver had hoped some of Sue's brand reputation would rub off on a gift bought elsewhere. Now *that's* a strong boutique brand!

Big brands need to spend a lot of money to get you to be loyal to them. As a boutique business, you have the opportunity to get that loyalty immediately—through one meaningful conversation, one unforgettable, earth-shattering experience, or one product that a customer couldn't possibly find anywhere else.

Your goal is to build a strong brand so you can charge more. You want your customers to be so impressed with your brand that they tell all their friends about you. You want your brand to give people a reason to shop, do business, or even wish to do business with you in the future. You want your brand to be so strong that people are willing to spend more money with you. You want them to do business exclusively with you, and complain that every other company isn't as fabulous as yours. It's about people being so excited that they talk about you and invest with you—that's the ultimate goal.

CHAPTER 1 ACTION STEPS

1. *Take out a sheet of paper and write down what your biggest fan thinks about your business. What's the coolest, most special thing about what you do? That should be the core of your brand.*

2. *Reach out to your ten biggest fans. Ask them what the coolest, most special thing is about what you do. Does it match what you said above? If not, you have some rebranding work to do, which we'll share how to do in chapter 3. If yes, great job! Now you'll learn more about how you can promote that.*

CHAPTER 2

Boutique Brand Essentials

WE ALL HAVE THOSE MAGICAL moments in life when we discover bliss. Erin had one when she stopped into Cupcake Joe's while in Portland, Oregon, on vacation and discovered a decadent chocolate cupcake. She was instantly hooked. And, four years later when she returned to Portland on a business trip, she knew she wasn't going to leave town until she stopped at Cupcake Joe's.

We've all found those obscure little shops that provide something amazing—they sit in the corner of our minds somewhere as a symbol of possibility. They show us how scrumptious chocolate cupcakes can be, or how completed we feel finding that obscure item that feels like it was designed specifically for us.

What happens when those special things change? What happens when you return to those businesses with an expectation, and you find a stale selection of cupcakes, a rude employee, fingerprints on the front door and the glass case, and crumpled-up receipts scattered around the counter? If this happened even once,

Erin probably wouldn't stop back in on her next trip to Oregon. (Fortunately, this wasn't her experience, and she'll be going back next time she's in town.) Basically, you, as a customer, lose your loyalty to that business. The brand—in other words, the way you feel about the business—changed.

Failing to get every single piece of a consistently mind-blowing experience right is where many small businesses fail when it comes to branding.

When Erin and I worked at an advertising agency, we regularly saw companies come in with inconsistencies in their brand. Most of what we saw was directly related to each company's identity.

Clients would bring in their advertisements, their promotional materials, and other branded items to our first client meeting to give us a chance to see where they had been. Sometimes we'd see five variations of a logo being used simultaneously (some of them were even clean, well-designed logos, but the variations still created inconsistencies). Or we would see numerous fonts within a logo or haphazard color schemes. Even the slightest change to a logo creates inconsistencies in identity and brand. It creates a disconnect with customers and prospects because of all those little inconsistencies, whether it's a sloppy logo or a disorderly bakery counter. And, this is also where the greatest opportunities exist for boutique businesses to beat their discounting competitors and charge what they're worth.

Your brand is worth more to the long-term success of your company than most other things. Don't hand it off just because you don't know how to manage it. You have the ability, unlike your thrifty competitors, to directly oversee the management of your identity and reputation with every single impression.

The bottom line is, your identity and brand are worth protecting. A strong brand creates consistency and a feeling of trust among your customers. It creates immediate recognition of your business.

"Your brand is worth more to the long-term success of your company than most other things. Don't hand it off just because you don't know how to manage it."

THE FIVE POINTS OF YOUR BOUTIQUE BRAND

The concept of building a strong brand—a brand that allows a boutique business to charge what it's worth—seems unattainable to many small business owners. However, by focusing on five simple points you can begin to build the foundation of a strong boutique brand.

1. Your Identity: How do people recognize you and your company? Think about it this way: the identity of your business is like your face. It's how people recognize you and know they can trust you. Your identity is more than just a logo. It's everything about your company, from your logo to your signage to your marketing pieces to how your location looks (if you have one) and your website. It's the foundation on which you build your brand and is truly the most important thing you have. So, your identity is how you look, and your brand is how people *feel* about you. If you change your face, people will not recognize you or immediately be able to determine what you stand for. Inconsistency in your business identity—a different logo in every application, mismatched fonts, or varying messages—can weaken your brand in an

> "Your identity is how you look, and your brand is how people feel about you."

instant. Customers won't recognize you and all the goodness you offer—the experience, the service, the customization, and the relationship—if your identity is marginalized, scattered, or conflicted. Your identity is the glue that holds your brand together. Here's the bottom line: you can't build a strong brand on a weak identity.

As a boutique business, you need to commit to building a strong brand, and that starts with your identity. We know that it's easier said than done. Many of you have tried this before. You've tried to improve your identity by having a better logo designed—with fancy new fonts and graphic elements that you think will draw more attention—but the problem is, slapping a new coat of paint on a cracked wall doesn't fix the problem; eventually, the cracks start showing again. In the next chapter, we'll show you how to fix a broken identity.

2. You Can't Please Everyone: If you aim to please everyone, you won't excite anyone—you become washed out and stripped of your personality. You can't fill every niche. You can't offer inexpensive, fast, customized, detailed, high-end, and everything else in between. Think about how generic some political figures become during elections because they want to please everyone.

> "Here's the bottom line: you can't build a strong brand on a weak identity."

They have to appeal to the masses to get elected. As a boutique business owner, you don't. So avoid the trying-to-please-everyone trap.

3. Your Reputation: If your reputation, personal or professional, is questionable, you risk losing the love and trust of your customers. As a boutique business owner, you must always have the highest integrity. It means that you pay attention to each detail of your offering, your identity, your attitude, your relationship with the public, and the outcome of every interaction and transaction. Your personal reputation, unlike the reputations of the leaders of most big chain stores, plays an enormous role in developing and strengthening your boutique business brand. Focus on your reputation. Manage it. Tweak it. And pay attention to it.

Your reputation is even more important as a boutique business because you *are* your brand.

> "Your reputation is even more important as a boutique business because you *are* your brand."

4. Your Consistency: At first glance, ultimate consistency might appear to be what the big-box brands have. McDonald's is the same no matter where you go—the logo is the same, the uniforms are the same, the food is the same, and the list goes on. Those golden arches are like a beacon in the night on a road trip, not necessarily because you love the food so much but because you recognize the symbol and you know what to expect—no surprises. Of course, McDonald's built that familiarity based on consistency. When you're a boutique business, brand consistency needs to be even more of a focus because you don't have that repetition. One off-brand or off-identity moment could create confusion or, even worse, damage the perception your customers have of your business. Your consistency as a boutique business has to be like that of a best friend—trustworthy, reliable, steady—because you have way fewer impressions with them.

What do you offer your clients, and what do they expect from you? Do you dazzle them with creativity? Are you the perfectionist? Do you offer something people can't find somewhere else? Or do you offer such personalized service that all your customers feel more like friends? This consistency is a primary factor in your brand—your customers know exactly what special things they can expect from you and your business.

The point is, without brand consistency, you won't get customer consistency. If there's a disconnect between what you say and what you do, or what you sell and how you market, or how you show the world your identity and how you serve people in reality, your customers won't know how to feel about you, and they surely won't know what to tell their friends about you.

5. Your Gush-Worthiness: Do people talk about you and your business? We're not talking about the buzz you would generate by engaging in promotional stunts like offering cleaning services with bikini-clad employees to get people talking. No, we're talking about the extraordinary things you do day in and day out. A running store might have a physical therapist on staff to help shoppers choose the right shoes to prevent injury. A small hospice facility might plant a tree with each patient when they arrive. Or a boutique baby shop might have walls decorated with handprints of each of its little customers in varying colors. All these simple things give customers a reason to talk about your business—they feel like they become part of it, that your business truly cares about them on a personal level.

CREATING STANDARDS FOR YOUR ENTIRE BRAND

Let's take a look at how you can create and enforce standards surrounding the five points of your boutique brand. This will build the foundation that affords you the opportunity to charge more.

Identity Standards

Your logo, signage, and promotional pieces are the external face of your company. Creating standards for your identity is critical. You want your audience to see your best light every single time they come in contact with you. You need to be a control freak about this. Here are some basic rules for keeping a consistent identity:

1. Hire a pro. Logos, signs, and graphics should only be designed by professionals. We know that can be expensive. But consider the fact that you'll spend $200 on a pair of jeans to enhance your personal identity. Are you really going to let a college kid, or your cousin who has some fun fonts and a copy of PhotoShop, design your business identity because he's free or really cheap?

2. Go for simple and timeless. Choose easy-to-read fonts instead of trendy fonts; otherwise, you'll look outdated in five years. Choose clean graphics and symbols to represent your brand. A fly-fishing outfitter in Idaho doesn't need a logo that has an image of a fish, a pole, the Grand Tetons, the Snake River, and a potato field. It's too much.

3. Give safe file formats. Ask your designer to send you your logos, trademarks, icons, and any other digital images in file formats that cannot be manipulated, reshaped, edited, or changed. When you send your logo out to be featured in an advertisement or at an event you've sponsored, you want to ensure that no one can squish it, change the colors, or do any other crazy thing to it. Your files also need to be scalable—so that they can be used in all sizes without getting pixilated or blurry.

4. Create an identity-standards manual. Take the time to create a living document or internal website that lists and states all the rules, fonts, colors, widths, etc., of your identity. This may sound like a tall order, but as your company grows, this identity-standards manual will allow you to police your brand without being involved in every single conversation. Employees, vendors, contractors, and partners will have a consistent reference point of your rules. Ask your graphic designer to create this for you. For an example, go here: www.wortheverypennybook.com/identitystandards.

5. Communicate your identity rules. Every time you send out something that represents your identity, attach your standards and agreements for usage, and ensure that all your employees do the same. Specifically state that any misuse or lack of compliance with these rules will result in the termination of any contract.

"You Can't Please Everyone" Standards

This is your opportunity to think about and filter all the excess stuff you do, sell, or offer that doesn't fit in your brand. It's your chance to cut the slack and focus on who you are and what really gets your core customers excited. This is the list of things *you will NOT do no matter what*. It will become one of the filters you use to make better decisions and protect your brand.

Some examples: "I will not donate my products or services to be raffled off at a golf tournament; golf tournaments attract men and my ideal client is female." "I will not add weddings to my photography business offerings just because there is demand; my focus and my passion is photographing children and babies." "As a contractor, I will not begin doing remodels just because a client has asked me to; my specialty is in designing homes from the ground up."

Reputation Standards

You need standards on how you manage your reputation. I choose not to have vanity plates on my vehicle because I am sort of a maniac driver. I really don't want people to recognize me when I'm swerving in and out of traffic, sailing through yellow lights, and squeezing into parking spaces too small for my large SUV. I know this won't have the most positive impact on my brand. If your business is just you, you can be sure to behave consistently to manage your reputation. But if you have employees out there representing you too, the need for reputation standards becomes pretty important.

Consistency Standards

Once you have a strong identity, the rule is simple: It's not about being the same most of the time. It's about being the same every time. Consider the expectations you've set for your customers. For example, maybe you've set the expectation that you will deliver orders in an hour or less, or that every single one of your products will be made from recycled materials. Some of you may have set the expectation that if customers have a problem—any problem—you'll make it right. Maybe you've told them that there's no place in town they can find the exact same thing your business offers. Whatever expectations you've set up, be consistent in fulfilling them. When you're consistent, you build trust and make your good clients want to talk about you and refer you.

Gush-Worthy Standards

Being on top isn't always easy. You have to keep raising the bar to thrill your loyal clients and get them talking about you to others. Can you empower your employees (or yourself) to do something unexpected for a different client each week as an added reason to gush about you? How far are you willing to go, and for which clients? That's what your gush-worthy standards need to include.

BE THE BRAND POLICE

Now that you've created your brand keeping these five points in mind, make sure to diligently watch over it. "Being the brand police" is, quite simply, the process of following the laws you've set in stone for your brand. Those laws are known as your brand standards. They are consistent laws for your identity and reputation. It's the process of defining how your brand will be seen and perceived no matter when, where, or how the public comes in contact with you—even at 6:00 a.m. on Saturday morning. And, even more importantly, it's the process of learning how to become a control freak about these standards—you can't allow yourself that one quick trip on Groupon or into the local clipper "just this once" to generate some "fast cash." Your brand can't afford it.

Years ago, I worked at a regional bottler of Coca-Cola Enterprises. The entire marketing department was given a massive, three-inch-thick book of every single brand inside the company—Coke, Diet Coke, Cherry Coke, Sprite, and so on. But when you're the little guy, there's no binder telling you how to use your logo to protect your brand. But you do need to know how to create rules for your identity and reputation that will inevitably build the consistency in your brand—so your customers know how to recognize you, why they love you, and what they'll tell their friends about your business the very next time they see them. Heck, they may even pick up the phone and call them immediately.

A FINAL NOTE ON BRANDING: WHY YOU'VE GOT TO GET IT RIGHT, RIGHT AWAY

When it comes building a strong brand, one that enables you to charge what you're worth, it's far more effective to do it right the first time rather than assume that there will come a point where you can climb into a cocoon, rebrand everything, and emerge as a butterfly.

Building a strong brand takes time. It just does. But creating standards for your identity, core offerings, reputation, consistency, and gush-worthiness will accelerate the process of becoming a strong brand.

Do you remember some of the most recognized brands when they were young? Nike, Google, Red Bull? What about Ralph Lauren, Facebook, True Religion, and MAC Cosmetics? These brands didn't just hop out the day they were born and become iconic. It took time. It took standards. It took a commitment to their products and a commitment to their identity. At first, all brands seem new and obscure—simply because they're unfamiliar. But, through time, they become beautiful.

As boutique business owners, we have a tendency to grip our revenue so tightly in the beginning that, in the end, our frugal nature becomes our worst enemy. But we're boutique. Our brands maintain our ability to charge more. If you think you don't have the time or resources to get your brand right the first time and commit to maintaining it over the next twenty years and beyond, then you probably won't have the resources for a redo any time in the future.

> "At first, all brands seem new and obscure—simply because they're unfamiliar. But, through time, they become beautiful."

But if you did do it all wrong and you need to start fresh, read the next chapter.

CHAPTER 2 ACTION STEPS

1. *Give yourself one week to perform an identity inventory. Lay out your marketing and promotional pieces and look for inconsistencies. If you identify any issues, hire a professional to help you pull it all together.*

2. *Create a living graphic-standards document. It should include the fonts, colors, and any other rules that should always be followed when it comes to your logo, marketing materials, etc.*

3. *Make a list of three things you want customers to remember every time they think of you, whether it's going the extra mile to find the perfect gift at the eleventh hour, or answering the phone to help a client in need after midnight, finding innovative solutions to their problems, or maintaining an uplifting supportive environment with every interaction.*

4. *What can you do to get people to gush over you? Make a list of what currently thrills your clients and sets you apart. What can you do more of? How can you take it to another level?*

CHAPTER 3

To Rebrand or Not to Rebrand?

THE DIRECTIONS ARE SIMPLE: Part A connects with Part D via Screw #8, with washer #11. See? You're already bored and frustrated.

We've met people who actually read the assembly directions that come with toys and furniture. Yes, it's a rare breed of people. Most of us simply want to grab all the parts and start sticking them together. And, sadly, that's what many small business owners do when they start the brand-building process (or their business).

As you've been reading the brand-assembly directions in the last chapter, are you realizing that maybe you did it all wrong? Is it too late to start over?

Before you start tearing the sign down from above your door—because now you hate your logo, or realize that your brand doesn't reveal your true personality, or realize that your brand is attracting an audience that wasn't necessarily your target—there are some extremely important things to consider.

Just ask some of our photographer friends who have rebranded how hard the process can be. Natalie has been in business for almost two years, and she's already rebranded twice. She says that she still hasn't found a logo that makes her 100 percent happy. But she doesn't want to wait too long to settle on one, fearing her current and future clients will not be able to connect her business with an identifiable brand.

Sandy purchased a studio she'd previously worked at. She created a new logo and identity that she and her colleagues liked, but it didn't communicate with past clients. Sandy is having issues almost two years later as she tries to recapture the studio's old business.

Clearly, rebranding isn't as simple as coming up with a few cool new concepts and implementing them. Before you rebrand, there are three key questions to consider. Let's take a look at them.

1. Are you rebranding for the right reason?

If you're rebranding simply because you no longer like the way your font looks or are just bored with the look of your logo, then it's time to slow down and reconsider. Dramatic changes to your brand just because you feel like spicing things up can create a really big mess. Keep in mind that just because you're bored with your logo doesn't mean everyone else is.

If you're wanting to rebrand because your margins are suffering, your customer base has dwindled, or a business you view as competition has opened, then this is a red flag. These not-so-shiny-or-desirable conditions can't be solved with a makeover of your brand. There's some deeper digging that needs to be done first to find the source of the issues. Rebranding because you're having business trouble is kind of like wearing black because you think it makes you look thinner. It might make you look thinner. But you're not actually thinner.

However, if you're wanting to rebrand because you haphazardly approached your identity when you started your business, or you acquired your business and the current brand is misleading, confusing, dated, or just plain bad, then it is the right time to consider rebranding. If you had a publicity issue that you couldn't overcome, such as declaring bankruptcy or having a huge product failure, it might also be time to consider rebranding.

2. How much brand equity will you lose?

Brand equity is the accumulation of all your marketing and advertisements, your public relations efforts, the experiences of your clients, the public's exposure to your logo, your donations to auctions and charities, your volunteer efforts, and your vendor relationships from when you started your business to now. Changing your brand might confuse your customers and the public. And although many businesses view rebranding as an opportunity to gain publicity and refresh their image (quite possibly attracting a new audience), it's a risky endeavor, because you could lose significant brand equity, the familiarity that you've already created.

Remember how confused you were when Prince changed his name to a symbol? Sure, he generated a ton of publicity, but did his album sales increase? Did anyone even recognize the symbol? What keys did fans type to find him on the Internet? Will your customers recognize you if you rebrand? Will they assume your company has been purchased or, worse, that you've gone out of business? And what are the aspects of your brand that you can't afford to lose? Could Donald Trump shave his head? What if Tiffany & Co. began to sell its products in a big-box store? What if Coke changed its formula? (Oh wait, they tried that . . .) Identify the specific things about your brand that people love and hold onto those things tightly.

3. How much are you willing to invest in your new brand?

If you're going to rebrand, you must go big. During my time in the advertising agency world, we helped an engineering firm rebrand. Because the company had changed and their admittedly out-of-date identity no longer reflected the forward thinking, energy, enthusiasm, and innovation it provided, its leaders decided to rebrand. Think about the investment it takes to change your brand on thirty years' worth of documents, uniforms, company vehicles, promotional items, signage, company literature, and countless other materials! But they went for it. And they went big. No longer was anything muted brown and gold; it was all sharp-contrast red, black, and white. The trucks were painted. All employees received new branded shirts. Absolutely everything was rebranded, and it clearly communicated to prospective clients the fresh, innovative spirit of the company. The effort was a massive success because it was embraced companywide. And at the end of the process, company leaders were glowing about all the new business, because the rebranding signaled to prospective clients that they were current and had fresh solutions.

Can you afford to embrace rebranding? Do a quick inventory and slap some price tags on rebranding before you make the commitment. How much will it cost to reprint all your promotional pieces? How much to rebuild your website? How much to rebuild your sign? How much will it cost to notify all your customers about your new identity? Everyone's inventory of costs will be different.

Consider every possible item that carries your brand and understand that they'll all need to be replaced simultaneously.

———

If all you're doing is slapping a new coat of paint on your crumbling foundation, rebranding is an expensive marketing idea that won't fix your problems, and the results will be short-lived. But if done correctly a rebranding strategy can breathe new life into your business, attract new customers, and create a buzz. Remember, rebrand for the right reasons and it can be a springboard to creating a business that's truly seen as worth every penny.

CHAPTER 3 ACTION STEPS

1. *If you're thinking about rebranding, sit down and honestly answer the three questions presented in this chapter: Am I rebranding for the right reason? How much brand equity will I lose? Am I willing to invest what it takes to make this rebranding initiative a success?*

2. *If you decide to move forward and rebrand your business, affix a dollar amount to the process. Get plenty of quotes. Have a trusted professional look at your numbers and give you feedback on how realistic they look. A half-executed rebrand is far worse than sticking with what you've got.*

3. *If you decide that rebranding is a viable strategy, set a hard date by when all of the old materials must be completely replaced.*

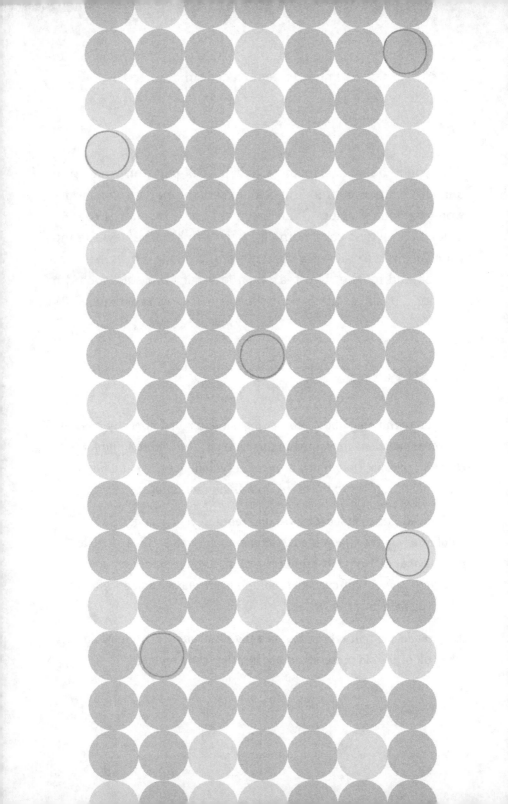

PRODUCTS, SERVICES, AND THE CUSTOMER EXPERIENCE

Now that we've explained the importance of investing in a strong brand to help you attract the right clients and increase the effectiveness of your future marketing activities, we're going to get into your offerings, and the high-touch customer experiences that surround them. When you're boutique, vanilla won't cut it. In this section, we will share stories of companies that have unbelievable products and services, backed with customer service that consistently delights their clients. (And you can bet that their prices reflect the quality they offer.)

But extraordinary products and top-notch service alone won't sustain your boutique business. In good times and bad, you have to keep the boutique filter firmly in place. We'll show the boutique way of handling problems when things go wrong. And if you get to the point where you're ready to expand, we'll also show you how to put together a staff made up of people who "get" your business.

CHAPTER 4

Making Boutique Products and Services Worth More

PHOENIX, ARIZONA, MIGHT BE HOME to one of the most unique hot dog restaurants you'll ever find. Imagine pineapple baked into the bun, and an all-beef dog grilled to perfection and smothered in homemade chili, then topped with coconut coleslaw. Maui Dog, as the restaurant is named, also offers toppings like mango, chipotle garlic mayo, and banana. These sound like odd flavor combinations, but the little hot dog restaurant is getting applause from snooty food critics for its surprising menu. And customers are raving about the little restaurant online like they've discovered a new staple in their diet.

But it's not just surprising or never-been-heard-of products that are deemed worth more than the average competitor's offerings.

Consider White House Custom Colour in the Minneapolis area. The professional photographic lab has been cheered and revered by the photography industry for its product mix for more than a decade. It's not because White House offers the most products or the cheapest products, but because its employees actually listen to their clients and develop new products based on their wishes. After the transition to digital photography, several top White House clients pushed for a more efficient solution to printing their clients' holiday cards in low quantities. White House made the investment, and, because their cards were a higher quality than their competitors, they attracted the clients who had higher quality standards. Clients asked for cool new photography backgrounds and White House responded. Clients wanted a place to purchase boutique bags that were sized for large framed photographs and White House took the request one step further by hiring a seamstress who could sew custom bags. Basically, White House has earned the "worth it" distinction and a tremendous amount of loyalty with its existing client base by creating cool products for its clients instead of only focusing on attracting new clients.

YOUR THRILL FACTOR

In order to truly stand apart in your industry, your products must make people go gaga over you. They need to be extra special, unmatched, interesting, or even shocking. A lighting store doesn't just sell switches and bulbs, but it might sell fixtures beyond compare and personalized consultation to help you amplify the natural light in your home. A gift basket business doesn't just sell fresh fruit and cheeses, but it might tailor each basket to the gift recipient—an anniversary basket may include wedding photos, "Our Memory of Your Wedding" cards filled out by close friends and family, or items from the resort where the couple spent their honeymoon.

The point is, your products, whether they be light fixtures or gift baskets, need to be special enough to make someone want to talk about them. And not just because of their price.

Consider Hound Comics, the only independently owned and operated comic book line available in Barnes & Noble. The company only produces one comic with limited spin-offs. Each book is full-color, thick, and includes the finest artwork. That description might sound like something offered by any comic book company, but it's not. Instead of the typically flimsy paper you'll find in the comic books produced by Marvel and DC, Hound Comics—despite being the little guys in the industry—prints its books on a magazine-grade paper. This costs the company more to print. In fact, when we spoke to the CEO, William "Brimstone" Kucmierowski, he explained the risk of printing on such high-quality paper, telling us that the company is not only spending more on the paper stock, but because they don't print as many books as the monster companies, the cost is even higher.

Why take such a risk? Brimstone told us that in order to compete, the company needed to create a reason to grab their comic book off the shelf amongst a sea of other choices. Because Hound Comics was the small independent company, they needed to create something more interesting than their competitors. Something more valuable. Sure it was a risk to invest more, but according to Brimstone, it's a risk that has definitely paid off, despite Hound Comics needing to charge more for each book. And Brimstone added that the fans are responding by saying that even though the book is a little pricier than others, it's definitely worth it for the way the illustrations and story pop off the page. Hound Comics is investing more and charging more, but the thrill factor is worth more.

So how can you make your offerings worth more? Here are the two primary ways to do it:

1. Seek the thrill. Instead of searching for ways to raise prices, slash costs, or become faster in order to compete with discounters, your sustainable competitive advantage is that you have the time and resources to find the gap—the empty place where you can add a thrill for the customer. In Dallas, there's a barbershop that offers patrons a beer while they wait to climb into the barber chair. In Salt Lake City, there's a tattoo artist who not only provides you with a mock rendering of your tattoo but who also takes your picture and PhotoShops an image of the tattoo onto your body so you can decide whether that tulip on your shoulder blade is in the perfect spot.

In Kansas City, there's a dry cleaner that beats the biggest brands by offering a more environmentally friendly cleaning process, along with pick-up and drop-off service to residents at no additional charge. They even have an annual Saint Patrick's Day tailgate in their parking lot for top customers. These are examples of simple things that show customers you want to provide a better experience. Look for that special something that can make you and your products different.

2. Make it impossible to emulate. The more customized your offerings are, the more difficult it will be for anyone to copy you, and your perceived value will continue to rise.

The harder it is for your competitors to copy you and your offerings, the more difficult it will be for them to compete with you. And when you make your product or service hard to copy, you also make it memorable—people want to talk about how great you are. And, more importantly, price is no longer their focus.

THE SECRET INGREDIENT IN YOUR BOUTIQUE BUSINESS: YOU

Your offerings reflect your passion for your business. They are a reflection of your brand. And they're probably the reason you started a boutique business in the first place—you wanted to make something better, more appealing, or more interesting. You wanted to create an experience for your clients that would give them a glimpse into why you find your craft so rewarding. In turn you've created a business.

Imagine completely remodeling your home with reclaimed materials—green building at its best. Your beautiful new wood flooring is made from hundred-plus-year-old railroad trestle wood that has been sitting at the bottom of the Great Salt Lake. Your baseboards are made from heat-treated scrap metal. Your cabinets are made from reclaimed sawdust. Even your insulation is made from recycled newspapers. Now imagine that all your furniture is custom built to suit your lifestyle. It's all handmade, and almost every material used was, at one time, used for something else. How much does the craftsman play a role in the end result of the remodel project? A ton, in this case.

Tim McCormac is the owner of Temac Development, a licensed commercial and residential contracting firm in California, Nevada, and Arizona. Tim is the driving force and creative energy behind the home described above. Customization and the use of reclaimed materials is Tim's passion. Although most customers who come to him for a remodel or complete build have a vague idea of what they want, most don't realize just how detailed their ideas can become when Tim turns them into reality.

How valuable is the "you factor" in your business? When everything is designed custom around you, your customers are pretty darned thrilled. If you are a service provider, you are the product yourself. You find the trestle wood that has been preserved by salt at the bottom of a lake for more than a hundred years. You find the scrap metal. And you turn it into the product for the customer. Other businesses might try to copy a lot of the things you sell. But they can't copy you, your ideas, your passion, and your ability to serve the customer.

> "Other businesses might try to copy a lot of the things you sell. But they can't copy you, your ideas, your passion, and your ability to serve the customer."

CHAPTER 4 ACTION STEPS

1. *Make a list of all your products and services. Look at which ones are vanilla or easily copied. Are they your most popular? Which offerings are most often cited as the reason people come to you? Can you get rid of some, or beef them up to make them more special and less easily copied?*

2. *Seek out other business owners in your community who are doing something that makes people rave about them. Get to know them and their businesses. Take them to lunch. Offer to help them so you can learn how they do what they do.*

3. Set a goal to find one area of your business each week where you can add value. Brainstorm with employees. Ask your vendors. And pay close attention to customer responses.

CHAPTER 5

The High-Touch Experience

DISCOUNTERS CAN'T COMPETE WITH YOU when you provide a better experience for customers. An experience they can't keep up with. One they can't touch. One that blows them out of the water. The boutique experience, and your ability to far surpass what discounters offer, gives you a huge advantage.

So, what does boutique service and experience really mean? Think about the last time you went to your local discounter. What did you experience that was brag-worthy when it came to the service or your shopping experience? You probably can't think of too many things—because in businesses that discount, "good service" and "a good experience" typically just mean that the customer wasn't disappointed.

As a boutique business you have a deeper relationship with your client. Therefore, instead of aiming for lack of disappointment (no hassles, no problems, and discounted prices), your goal is to move beyond simple satisfaction. You should provide services and experiences that thrill customers. You should spend more time with each client, giving them those high-touch, personalized experiences.

It's contractors like Tim McCormac who truly realize that your home is your castle. He's there with you along the way, asking how you live and what you prefer. He sees that you have a dog and proposes a hidden doggie door. He notices that you collect vintage movies and proposes a screening room in the extra bedroom.

When Erin was coaching cross country at Lincoln College in Lincoln, Illinois, she was in charge of buying running shoes for the team. She called the Springfield Running Center and the owner, Derrick Dexheimer, brought his entire inventory to her. He drove it all thirty miles so that her entire team could get the perfect-fitting running shoes. Sure Erin got offers from many other retailers for shoes at a cheaper price, but for her the service of having her athletes custom-fit for their shoes was more valuable. A large retailer like Foot Locker would never do that. With their discounts, they can't afford to.

The point is, wanting to merely satisfy customers is kind of like saying, "We won't do anything wrong." But giving customers boutique service is like saying, "We're going to build the best relationship with you by doing the things you would never ask us to do."

Moving your service and experience beyond just satisfying customers means you're focusing on the future, not the past. Instead of focusing on whether your service was satisfactory, the boutique business owner focuses on building the relationship so that everything will continually become more and more fantastic.

Moving beyond satisfaction starts with knowing your customers and their desires. But, beyond just knowing them, you need to be prepared to blow their minds with every little bit of attention. Consider Just For Pets, an Austin, Texas, pet boutique and groomer. The owners pride themselves on knowing every dog's name and greet each canine customer with treats when they arrive. They also keep a database of which pets received which hairstyles so customer pooches can get the same snazzy style each and every time, no matter which groomer is holding the shears. Customers

> "The point is, wanting to merely satisfy customers is kind of like saying, 'We won't do anything wrong.' But giving customers boutique service is like saying, 'We're going to build the best relationship with you by doing the things you would never ask us to do.'"

all feel as if their dog is the favorite—even if their dog barks the entire time she's getting clipped. Yet, Just For Pets surpasses the concept of knowing its customers. Our friend, Kris Pauls, is a client of Just For Pets. Kris likes to pamper her pooch, Maybelline, a schnauzer/terrier mix. Maybelline only has one eye, and the groomers know just how to style Maybelline's hair—leaving one side of the hair around her face a little longer so that it covers her missing eye but still looks natural.

Or consider how Simplicity Sofas, a boutique furniture company, provides personalized service to customers even though 95 percent of its business transactions happen online.

The company's niche is "furniture that fits"—quality sofas and furniture for small spaces. Its ideal client is people who have skinny doorways or stairwells or are challenged in the amount of space they have to live in. Simplicity Sofas has turned a potential low-touch online concept into a service- and experience-oriented success. There's a hotline that customers can call after hours and reach a live person. The company insists on a minimum of ten email or phone contacts with the client between the first contact with the company and the delivery of the product; they want to make sure everything is perfect. Then, Simplicity Sofas calls every single customer after delivery to make sure absolutely everything about the product, the delivery, and the service is beyond satisfactory.

Owner Jeff Frank learned how to make online customer service high touch through his experience volunteering with a consumer advocacy group, A Call to Action. The nonprofit's goal is to help consumers who feel they've been wronged in a business transaction—whether it's a faulty product, a strange mishap, or a dispute over an invoice.

Jeff says that during his time with A Call to Action he realized some strangely simple truths:

1. When companies do nothing to resolve an issue with a customer, the customer becomes extremely angry.

2. When a company does something to fix the problem, the customer typically forgives the company.

3. When a company goes above and beyond—not just fixing the problem but doing something to truly delight them—customers will not only forgive the problem but will forever be company fans.

Jeff realized that customer service—to the extreme—is far more effective than advertising, and it costs a lot less.

Hundreds of thrilled customers have written testimonials to Simplicity Sofas, and the company has been removed from numerous online ranking sites because the algorithms view the purely positive feedback as a hoax! Anyone who Googles Simplicity Sofas and will have a hard time finding any negative reviews on any site. And Jeff says that his goal to make every single customer happy even applies to those who return their orders—he wants them to be thrilled that even the return process was fantastic. That's over-the-top service and experience.

At Sarah Petty Photography, the experience we provide is one of our biggest sustainable competitive advantages. Recently, a family with seven kids came in for a portrait session. We put fake mustaches on each one of the family members. They were cracking up and having fun as a family. When it came time to order, they ordered a large framed portrait of the mustache images to hang in their home. Every time they come in, they still talk about how much fun it was. Who thinks of getting a family photo taken as family bonding time? It's a conversation and a family memory they'll have for years.

This is where boutique businesses have the opportunity to truly blow away their competitors. It's through the service—not only making sure your customer is satisfied, but making sure they're thrilled. It's through the experience—making it fun to do business with you and giving people an emotional reason to want to come to you. Make it worth talking about. Connect with customers and step into their shoes.

This is why you can charge higher prices. You make sure the service and experience thrills your customers to the point that price isn't the focus.

WHAT ARE THE TRADEMARKS OF A HIGH-TOUCH EXPERIENCE?

When you're giving customers the high-touch experience that is the hallmark of a truly successful boutique business, you'll notice that the following is true:

1. Customers feel as if they're being treated as an individual, and the boutique business is focused on delivering a service customized to their personal desires.

2. The relationship is a two-way street. The customer is willing to pay more because the boutique is willing to offer a more personalized, "in your best interest" level of service. The customer knows they're getting more from you, and that costs more.

3. Both the customer and the boutique are excited to do business together. The experience is worth it, and the boutique actually wants to see the customer delighted.

4. Customers feel as if they're your favorite client. Each and every time they enter, they are greeted like a long lost friend.

BOUTIQUE BOUNDARIES

In order to consistently deliver an amazing high-touch experience for your clients, you need to set boundaries. In fact, boundaries can be an advantage. Obviously, if your business makes custom products for customers, your turnaround time will be longer than a company that sells off the shelf. If your business sells personalized or one-of-a-kind items, your guarantees are likely going to be customized to the client's need. And you definitely need boundaries if you *are* the product—the relied-upon consultant, the copywriter who "is the voice" of your customer, or the guitar teacher who knows how to inspire the kid who is easily distracted. You can't be working around the clock or you will be depleted and unable to perform with a passion; your customers must follow the rules of your schedule. Although all of these rules might initially seem like you're providing a lesser service, they may actually be creating a deeper relationship and a higher demand for your boutique business.

Consider Gordy's Hi-Hat, a boutique burger joint in Cloquet, Minnesota. The restaurant recently celebrated more than half a century in business. Given that the restaurant sits on the edge of a small town on the way to even smaller towns, Gordy's Hi-Hat continues to be a destination for travelers. What is Gordy's biggest rule of business? The restaurant is only open during the summer months. In fact, ask anyone who lives or travels through Northern Minnesota about the local signs of summer's arrival. It's not a groundhog—it's the opening of that little burger joint on the hill.

Or consider the rules established by Matt Look, who owns Fortis Designs, a graphic design and web design studio in Idaho Falls, Idaho. Matt works around the clock for his clients—nights, weekends, and even on some holidays. However, he has made it a rule that he stops working every day between the hours of 4:30 p.m. and 8:30 p.m. to have dinner and spend quality time with his family. No phone calls, no emails, no conference calls. The middle of the night is fine with Matt. Just don't expect to reach him during his family time.

HOW DO YOU ESTABLISH RULES FOR YOUR BOUTIQUE BUSINESS?

1. Align with your big picture. You're boutique and you are in business because you are passionate about your craft and offer the world something better or different. Your rules have to align with your big picture. If Gordy's Hi-Hat customers begged and begged for the restaurant to remain open all year long and the owners bent on their rules, it may not be the raging success it is today. In fact, it may no longer exist. The truth is that Gordy always loved spending winters in Florida—that was his big picture. He got a reprieve from the frigid winters of Northern Minnesota. He was able to rejuvenate, refocus, and come back in the springtime ready to work like a madman.

2. Manage customer expectations. Yes, you're going to give your clients over-the-top treatment. But when you establish rules, it's a must to communicate those rules. Tell your customers that you don't accept calls during family time. Tell them that you take Friday afternoons off to train for marathons. Tell them that you don't offer lesser quality or faster turnaround or overnight anything, because it affects the overall integrity of your brand. Managing your customers' expectations allows you to develop a relationship of understanding with your customers. Let them know why you have certain rules. Customers will most often respect your rules when they understand the reasons for those rules. You can't be open twenty-four hours, but you will give them ten times the service and experience when you are open. Your customers will respect you for having rules that enable you to provide an extreme level of service. They'll notice when you're excited about—not exhausted by—their business. They'll love it when you're thinking about them in your free time rather than avoiding them because you have no free time.

―――

When you find the thrill factor, those things that make your clients stand up and cheer for you, you've achieved one of the necessities of a boutique business. Go beyond any fathomable expectation your customer can have for your business, and you'll be able to charge what you're worth and thrill your clients at the same time.

CHAPTER 5 ACTION STEPS

1. *What are some of the ways you can thrill your clients? Sit down and write down everything that comes to mind.*

- *Can you deliver your product or service in a way that nobody else can or does?*

- *Can you customize something further than you already are?*

- *Can you make life easier for your client in any way?*

- *Can you make your client look good to their friends and family?*

- *Can you solve a problem they don't know they have?*

2. What are the boundaries you're going to set for yourself as a boutique business owner? Write down what you will and won't do for your customers, and share them with your employees if you have any. Remember, your boundaries must:

- align with the big picture of your business

- set up realistic customer expectations and protect your own sanity

- be balanced by over-delivering in other areas of your business that fall within your boundaries

CHAPTER 6

Building a Team That Completes the Boutique Experience

WE ALL KNOW THIS FEELING—SOME people in our lives we could live without even if we like them, but with other people we have an instant connection. Not a romantic connection, but a love for a shared passion. As a boutique business owner, you need to pay attention to the pitter-patter you feel when you meet someone who shares the same enthusiasm and passion as you. When you meet those people who you trust and admire, keep them in mind as potential team members.

As a boutique business, if you need help in your business, you're probably not going to recruit employees like most businesses do. And you shouldn't. The big-box stores can manage trial periods. They have a team to train people. They can move people who aren't a great fit to a different department. And they can afford to make a few hiring mistakes. You can't afford it. If someone has a negative experience at Target because of a rude employee, it is unlikely to stop them from returning to the store. If, however, they experience a rude employee at a boutique business, they will most likely judge you more harshly—they pay you more because you're supposed to give them an outstanding experience.

As a boutique business, if you have one employee, that person's interaction could make up 100 percent of the customer's experience. Your employee could change the way your customers perceive you, trust you, talk about you, and do business with you.

Your team needs to represent your brand entirely.

> "Your team needs to represent your brand entirely."

HOW TO BUILD YOUR DREAM TEAM

Because so much rides on the people you choose to sell your products or carry out your services, we've put together these six steps for building a dream team—one that will wow your clients every time.

1. Look for passion. When you're looking for employees, look for the most passionate people—the ones who love what you do. Keep your eye out for these people everywhere, even as you're doing business: some of your best customers may also make great team members. Your passionate customers already know what you sell, how you sell it, and how you serve your clients. Plus, they've already shown an interest in you, your products, or your services and come to you without needing a discount. The fact that they gush about you on their own time makes them the best possible salesperson for your business! Look for an opportunity to work more closely with them—on a project, volunteering together, etc.—to see if they might be a good fit for your business. You can train people for skills, but you can't train people to have glowing personalities and a love of people and relationships. You can't train them to be driven. And you surely can't train them to care about your business as much as you do. Seek the passion first, and deal with all the other stuff later.

2. Don't skimp. Because you're not discounting your prices, you have higher margins and can afford better people. Pay for better people and you'll get better results. Don't base your employees' wages on how much the discounters pay their people. If you hire the right people and treat them well, they will enable you to do more business. And, boutique businesses have the advantage of employing team members who care about more than a dollar figure. There are people who could be fabulous employees but maybe don't want the commitment or structure of a corporate gig. They want to be in a cool environment with cool people. The want a flexible schedule so they can travel or work only while their kids are at school. They want special benefits of your offerings—on the photography, clothing, spa services, etc.

3. Don't settle. Choosing employees for your boutique is much like choosing a mate: good enough just isn't going to be good enough. The right team members will excite you. They should embody your brand—from how they look and dress to how they speak and communicate with those around them. Good enough—even if you plan for just a temporary position—can do mega-damage to your brand, and can be emotionally exhausting. Ask your friends and clients for their opinions, too. Get references. See if those around you are as excited as you are about the prospective employee.

4. Filter, filter, filter. All of these points might be sending chills up your spine and making you anxious about hiring the right people. That's good. You should be just as terrified about hiring the wrong people as you are excited about hiring the right people. Filter your potential employees well before you offer anyone the job. And as you filter, realize that you need to look at all their skills—not just those that relate to the job function. Boutique businesses need well-rounded, passionate employees. An employee at a boutique IT firm might write fantastic code, but can he provide service to customers with your standards of interaction in mind? Can he write grammatically correct emails to business accounts? Think through all the touch points your employees will have with your customers. And when someone gets through your filter, hold on to her for dear life!

5. Treat them like family. Just as you treat your good clients like friends, you should treat your boutique employees like family. A close, supportive working environment allows you to customize your rules to the needs of each member of your team. Employees with children may need flex time. If the job involves intense focus, the employee may need quiet and may work more efficiently from home. Look for opportunities to support each of your teammates in their personal growth. Whether they want to take time off to go to college or train for a marathon, as a boutique business, you have the flexibility to help your employees achieve their goals and make them happier while they're at work.

6. Become a role model or mentor. Becoming a mentor will not only help someone who is just starting out; it will also teach you a lot about yourself, your business, your brand, and the world. Plus, when you are open to this, people who are passionate about what you do will enter your life. In fact, our business partnership started with a one-day job-shadowing experience many years ago. Erin sent a note to me at the ad agency while she was in college and asked to shadow me for the day. She is now my business partner. Andria, the production manager at Sarah Petty Photography, also originally started as a job-shadower and worked her way into an intern position. She then worked her way into a full-time position. I didn't go into either of those situations looking for employees—much less a business partner. But, when those special people pop into your life, look for opportunities to work with them more closely.

With the right team behind you, you know with confidence that your customers are being cared for, and that they'll continue to invest in your superior products, services, and experience. And you might even free up a good deal of your own time, giving you room to come up with ways to make your growing boutique business even more incredible.

CHAPTER 6 ACTION STEPS

1. *If you're in the market for a new employee (perhaps your first), keep your eye out for people who give you that feeling of instant connection.*

Remember, they can crop up anywhere, so keep an open mind, whether you're catching up with an old friend, serving as a mentor, or checking out at the grocery store.

2. If you need to actively seek out employees, set aside a couple of hours to get clear on the roles and responsibilities that you need.

3. Reach out to your network to let them know you have a job opening before advertising it in the newspaper. There are often good people right under your nose, and you'll save a lot of time and effort sifting through resumes of people who aren't qualified and don't understand what you do. When you tap into your network, you have a better chance of attracting the smart, devoted, relationship-savvy type of person who appreciates what you do.

CHAPTER 7

When the Boutique Experience Goes Wrong

TONY OWNS A CUSTOM CABINET and furniture business. In his city, he's known as the guy who builds benches in nooks and storage in kitchens to match his customers' preferences and lifestyles.

A recent job had him remodeling a restaurant patio with custom seating so his client—the owner of the place—could make the best use of the natural scenery in a small space. Tony was elated to start the project.

The seating was built. Custom beams were erected to hold sun-screening. And now Tony was ready to paint. The client had requested numerous colors. It was a complex color scheme. Tony had pre-painted as many pieces as possible before installation, but due to the customized nature of the patio he had to reserve some painting for touch-ups upon completion—blue here, red there, lime green over there.

Touch-ups were estimated to take about two hours, and Tony was trying to move as fast as possible because he noticed an unexpected cloud in the distance. Within minutes, sprinkles began falling from the sky. And due to the odd shape of the patio, tarps would only cover a portion.

Then came heavy rains and winds. It was nasty. And so were the new blended colors of the patio. He'd end up having to redo the whole project.

Who is at fault? No one.

Tony had checked the forecast. He had informed the client of a chance of rain that evening. And, together, they had decided to move forward with the project that day.

Situations like these happen all the time in business. And when they do, they create the perfect opportunity for a boutique business to step up. Think about it. If you can overcome a negative situation with a customer, you take that customer beyond basic satisfaction. Now they're not displeased—they're thrilled.

Tony understood that he was sitting on an opportunity. He laid out a plan to remedy the situation. He asked the bar owner which night of the week was the slowest night. He then asked whether he would be willing to close off the patio for one full night so Tony could host a private painting party—inviting his painter friends to help him finish the job in a timely manner while Tony supplied his crew with dinner before the job and an open tab (on Tony) after the job was finished. Although the bar owner knew Tony's tab for the evening wouldn't compare to the revenue generated from the public, he liked the idea because he knew that even if the patio had been painted during the day, he would have to close it to customers. The job was finished in one night and the relationship was on solid ground.

Early in my small business career, I attended a business program by renowned author, speaker, and customer service guru John DiJulius. That was the first time I heard the phrase, "It's not your fault but it is your problem." I've clung to that statement ever since. As photographers, physicians, artists, retailers, craftsmen, trainers, hairstylists, and chefs, we know that problems can arise, without fault. Nevertheless, fault or no fault, the problems will still exist, and they need to be overcome. If clients aren't thrilled, if they have to settle, if they don't receive the best service, product, and value, then they can't brag about your business. As a boutique business, overcoming or addressing problems is not only a responsibility—it's also an opportunity.

Consider what happens at a big-box business if there's a problem. You call an 800 number that rings to a call center, and a representative tells you the company policy regarding your problem. It's not service, though. They aren't problem solvers. They just explain company policy. And you hope the policy comes out in your favor.

In a boutique business, there's not a policy manual to cover every problem, and we usually don't have the time or money to find adequate substitutes for our custom products. Our products are matchless. So how do we handle problems?

> "It's not your fault, but it is your problem."
> —John DiJulius

1. View the customer as a friend. The most important thing to remember when handling mistakes, whether it's your fault or not, is to focus on maintaining the relationship. You wouldn't look at a friend and say, "Deal with it, it's not my fault." No—you'd ask how the situation can be resolved. Remember, you're a boutique business, and strong relationships are a huge part of what you offer. Because you've established "worth it" prices that give you the financial freedom to remedy any situation that may arise, own the relationship. Treat the customer like a friend you don't want to disappoint. Make good on any bad situation. In fact, make *great* on the situation.

> "As a boutique business, overcoming or addressing problems is not only a responsibility— it's also an opportunity."

2. Ask for ideas. Solutions that might make you happy aren't necessarily what will make your customer happy. Ask what you can do to make the situation right. Often it's less than what you would have offered.

3. Seek the opportunity. Most customers will look past mistakes as long as you own them, show intent to fix them, and are transparent and clear about the process, cost, and time associated with the remedy. For example, Tony explained to the restaurant owner the process for fixing the paint problem, how long it would take, and that he was willing to remedy the situation. The bar owner appreciated the fact that Tony was not only willing to make it right, but also that Tony realized the bar owner's situation and proposed a plan that was more helpful to all parties.

4. Seek negative feedback. We understand how great it feels to have customers who rave about your business, but negative feedback is actually more valuable than positive feedback. Granted, it's often hard to find. That's why you need to make a point of searching for negative feedback. If you run into a negative situation with a client, talk to him.

The people who might be upset or displeased are much more likely to give you perspective on how you can improve your business. It's a valuable perspective that your biggest fans can't provide. You need to hear the negative so you can ensure that what one customer feels isn't being felt by all customers. Denying there's something negative out there doesn't mean it's not out there. Set Google alerts for your name and the name of your business. Ask employees and vendors to please tell you if they hear negative comments. And when you find the negative stuff, use it as an opportunity to bounce back. Don't automatically become defensive, and be sure to let your customer know that you value their honesty even if you don't agree with them. Personally reach out to the parties who are unhappy with you and make good.

> "Denying there's something negative out there doesn't mean it's not out there."

WHAT HAPPENS WHEN YOU MAKE A MISTAKE AND IT IS YOUR FAULT?

Okay, so you really blew it. It's all your fault. There was no sudden rainstorm. You can't blame Mother Nature. How do you remedy the situation? No one likes excuses. Even though customers don't always like hearing the truth, they'll generally respect you for it.

Here's our favorite "oops" moment from Sarah Petty Photography.

A customer had requested a huge wall portrait. A few months before placing the order, she sent in the measurements of the space where the piece would hang. But when it came time to choose the size, all we heard was "Let's make it huge!" So we did. In our excitement we ordered the largest frame available and didn't even check the previous measurements. Yeah, oops. The portrait she received was way too big.

The client didn't panic, though. We had already built a strong relationship, so she knew I would fix the problem no matter what it took. It was late on a Friday when I learned about the problem. I personally called the client to apologize and let her know that we knew of the problem and didn't want it to ruin her weekend. She said that she knew we would take care of her and wasn't worried about it. The next week, we had a courier service drive ninety miles to pick up the artwork, because it was too large to fit in any of our vehicles. We promptly had the frame chopped down, reordered the photo, and had it sent back to her.

How do you resolve problems that are all your fault? Here are three simple rules to follow when it comes to making good on your mistakes.

1. Own it. Make it a rule that you will make good and never leave the client hanging. Notify customers of problems the moment you know about them, and never leave a client struggling to fix the problem on her own.

2. Ask first. Start by first asking the client how they would like to see the situation resolved. They like to hear that you're opening the door to their needs and desires. Your customers have chosen to do business with you because they're impressed by other things you have done. And more often than not, the remedy they request will be far less expensive than the remedy you are willing to provide.

3. Be prepared to do whatever it takes. If there is no possible way to remedy the situation without a refund, be prepared to refund their investment. Yes, it may be financially painful in the short term, but this is a case where the long term is much more important.

CHAPTER 7 ACTION STEPS

1. *Develop a system to consistently ask your customers for negative feedback. It won't be pleasant to hear (and some customers may be reluctant to give it to you), but it will be invaluable in helping you avoid future mistakes and better resolve the ones that do happen. For example, "I'd love to hear if there was anything I could have done better to thrill you."*

2. *Make it a point to set up a fund for when things do go wrong so that your decision on how to fix the mistake isn't clouded by you not having the money to do the right thing. Make sure your response can always be "Yes, we will fix it."*

PRICE

....

Pricing is definitely the scariest part about owning any small business. We love what we do. We are passionate about thrilling our customers. But then that guilt creeps in—we don't want people to think we are being greedy.

Every day we are in business, we take risks. We pay insurance, we commit to rent or a mortgage so that others can profit. The entire burden of survival falls upon our shoulders.

In this section, we'll look at how to set your prices, how *not* to set your prices, and how discounting can damage your brand (with some notable exceptions).

CHAPTER 8

Price Isn't Everything

IMAGINE YOURSELF ON A BEACH somewhere along the coast of the south Caribbean. The crystal blue water is gently massaging your toes with each wave. From a nearby grass hut you hear the pleasantly steady thump of reggae.

You scan the beach from end to end. It's not jammed with vacationers or college kids. It's perfect. It's everything you had wanted on vacation but could never seem to find before this trip because you don't have the expertise and were trying to save a buck.

As your toes rake through the white sand, you realize how much better this trip is compared to last year's vacation, which you booked yourself. Last year's trip was filled with overcrowded places, long lines, beaches crawling with vendors, and marginal service at the hotel. Despite being skeptical about paying more for professional travel advice, now you see the difference, and you owe all your gratitude to your travel agent.

A lot of you might be thinking, *Yeah right, a travel agency made that much of a difference? Didn't those all die when Priceline.com came around?* (Let's face it, Captain Kirk was an irresistible pitchman.) Or maybe you thought travel agencies couldn't survive after 9/11, when travel as we knew it changed forever. Or maybe you thought the Internet itself—not just Priceline.com—slowly plucked away at the entire concept of the travel agency because research, planning, and booking travel became so user-friendly.

All of these factors did leave quite a scar on the travel industry. However, they also illustrate one really fantastic point, which, as a boutique business operator, you must know—the travel agencies that tried to compete on price are the ones that died. They didn't have to beat the prices of Priceline or Travelocity. They didn't have to lower their margins, because they operated on a different level. They had a value-driven business model, a well-branded identity, and an extreme service orientation to each customer.

Quite simply, those agencies that survived did so because they made their offering worth a price that enabled them to stay in business, unlike the agencies that tried to compete on price.

Consider Kahalla Travel out of San Diego—an agency that not only survived the shift in consumer travel but thrived by not competing on price.

Becky Gillespie, a travel specialist at Kahalla Travel, told us that she goes out on a limb to add special touches to her clients' trips. For instance, a client named Libby booked a fiftieth birthday party trip to the Dominican Republic with her girlfriends. Knowing Libby's actual birth date, Becky called both the sales manager and the hotel manager at the Dominican Republic property and asked if they could do a little something special for the client, including decorating Libby's room and providing a surprise cake. Libby's friends were amazed, and Libby couldn't stop talking about how special she felt thanks to Becky.

Becky also told us about a client who hadn't booked with Kahalla in a long time. The couple called and asked to be booked on a specific Mediterranean cruise. Basically, this couple had already planned their trip and just wanted the agency to make the actual booking for them. But after talking with the couple, Becky found out that the husband was a recently retired theology professor. So, putting on her boutique-business thinking cap, Becky dug in to provide more value. She knew she had an entire jump drive full of walking tours and maps of Christian sites in Rome. She sent it to them so they could check out the sites before their cruise departed. Without a doubt, the client was thrilled, and the experience Becky provided solidified their loyalty to Kahalla Travel.

Does all this sound like just great service? Of course it does. But it's the very thing that allows you, as a boutique business, to stay away from price competitions. It takes the emphasis off price and attracts clients who value what you do for them.

> "Quite simply, those agencies that survived did so because they made their offering worth a price that let them stay in business."

PRICE WARS: BEHIND THE SMILEY FACE

What happens to your business when a company like Walmart, Sears, Kmart—or even a person who started a business out of her home—brands itself as the lowest price in town and then attaches that big yellow smiley face, a gigantic SALE sticker, or a blue light to the price tags? What happens when the big-box stores offer massive inventory, open doors 365 days a year at all hours, and national brands at prices that continue dropping? What happens when a business somewhere across the nation or even overseas busts into your customer base via the Internet, by offering a ridiculously low price? Oh, and what happens when a home-based business owner—who is pursuing their hobby and doesn't care about profit—enters your market and offers everything for next to nothing?

What happens to your business, your customer base, your revenue, and your profits when any business undercuts you on price? If you're truly boutique, you're sitting on a goldmine of opportunity—you are following a different business model based on everything we're teaching you in this book.

The Internet, big-box stores, and low-price local stores don't make it impossible to compete in your marketplace, but they do make it impossible to compete on price. You can't and shouldn't pursue this strategy. As a boutique business, you don't offer the same products. You don't offer the same level of service. You might not offer twenty-four-hour service, or even speedy service. And you shouldn't offer the lowest prices—if your margins are that tight, you can't afford to stay in business, because you can't afford to do special things. Just like Kahalla Travel, you offer something better, and people are willing to pay for it. Yes, you come with "worth it" products that people will pay more for. And no, you aren't for everyone.

Your prices allow you to give more attention to customers, and to your ongoing relationship with them. Because you aren't serving everyone in town, you have time to find out exactly how to treat them on their birthday. Your prices allow your customers pride in ownership of the products they buy from you because your name is on it and your passion is behind it. What you do is "brag-worthy." Your customers talk about you so *you* don't have to talk about you.

Take the Duluth Grill in Duluth, Minnesota. Its menu includes vegetarian, gluten-free, healthy options as well as homestyle comfort foods. Everything is homemade. However, what makes the Duluth Grill so special is how they design their menu and cuisine around local produce and meats. In fact, the Duluth Grill actually has its own garden on the premises and during the summer months offers customers "just picked" entrees. Are the prices higher than other big-box franchises in the area? Shouldn't they be?

It all boils down to the fact that as a boutique, you don't offer the same thing as your discounting competitor. So you shouldn't be offering the same price. If you do, you'll undercut your own worth in the eyes of consumers and weaken your business's financial strength in the process. Should your offerings be worth the prices you charge? Definitely.

CHAPTER 8 ACTION STEPS

1. *Write down what it is about your business that allows you to charge more than your competitors. This is what we call your sustainable competitive advantage (remember, price isn't sustainable). Focusing on this aspect of your offerings will keep you confident in the premium prices you charge for your premium products.*

2. *Make a list of businesses you use that you pay more for. It may be your auto repair garage, bakery, child's dance studio, restaurant, or carpet cleaner. What do they do that makes you willing to pay more? Can you incorporate any aspect of that into your business?*

CHAPTER 9

The Boutique Pricing Strategy

AS A BOUTIQUE BUSINESS, HOW do you put a price tag on the time you spend with your clients, the attention to detail that you give, the passion you put into every product you create or service you offer?

You could take a high-level class on pricing, or read a six-hundred-page manual that takes a degree in rocket science to understand. But most of us don't have the time or energy to get into those kinds of details. We're busy working on our craft, art, talents, and businesses. To succeed with the boutique business model, you have to at least understand the basics of pricing—*then* you can spend all those long hours in tying bows into swan shapes, stirring up grandma's secret tortilla recipe, or creating illustrations on your handmade drink coasters.

Determining the price of your offerings can seem frightening. You might be thinking that you don't want to undercut yourself, or maybe you're afraid of overpricing to the point where you won't get many customers. So where do you start? How do you establish prices that will bring you a profit but also keep your customers saying, "It's worth every penny!"?

I remember being unsure about pricing when I first opened my photography studio. It's natural for new business owners to struggle with pricing. In my case, I was turning something I was doing as a hobby, photographing kids, into a business. So the realization struck me that if I was going to leave my babies to create heirloom artwork for other people's babies, I wanted to earn at least what I would in a traditional career. And, beyond that, I also knew that producing the art I wanted to create for customers wasn't a turn-and-burn business. I couldn't just capture the magic in each child or that relationship with her parents in a seven-minute photo session. I had to spend more time with each client to achieve the style of photography that had already created a demand for me. That meant making my time worth more. I needed to charge for that extra time and attention because I was in business to make a profit.

For all boutique businesses, pricing can be a tricky discussion—especially when you first start out. But if you want to stay in business and afford to do all of the special things you do for your clients, you must get your prices right.

HOW **NOT** TO SET YOUR PRICES

We want you to think about pricing differently. It isn't about spending weeks analyzing every penny (although we rely heavily on our numbers to make decisions). It is about understanding the concepts and having the confidence to know that you can charge what you are worth. Here are three traditional approaches to setting prices that we don't advise using:

"The Big Guess": Okay, so let's not even consider this a strategy, but we had to include this approach because we see so many boutique (especially creative) businesses that use it. Some don't know the value of their time, don't know their costs, don't know anything other than that they love what they do. They're simply happy that someone is willing to pay them to do their craft, and often leave the pricing up to the customer. Or worse, they negotiate with the customer because they aren't confident with their pricing structure. Unless you happen to get lucky, which is doubtful, this method of setting prices won't make you profitable.

Competitive-Based Pricing: Many new businesses base their prices on those of their competitors, but if you use this as a boutique business, you are going to get into huge trouble. If you owned a web design firm and didn't know how much to charge for the creation of a website, you might go online to check up on what other designers are charging. The problem, of course, is that you would find web design services ranging in price from $100 to $50,000. You'd then narrow the search to find companies that offer comparable service to yours. If you're using this pricing strategy, you're trying to justify the price of a product as if it's a commodity, with no regard for your operating expenses, the relationships you build with customers, or the value of your time, service, perspective, and expertise. As a web designer looking at your competitors, you don't know their business model. You don't know whether they're skilled, whether they're selling custom sites or merely templates, whether they're offshoring or outsourcing a lot of the work. Do they have a team of people dedicated to creating focus group–tested sites? Not to mention you don't even know if they are operating a profitable business. Not knowing what goes into the creation of your competitors' sites, why should you assume that you need to be competitive with their pricing? Competitive pricing can be effective for high-volume businesses that sell commodities. But you're not a high-volume business selling a commodity, so you will get burned if you set your prices based on the competition.

Cost-Based Pricing: Okay, so most of you creative types are going to hate this portion because it includes math, but we'll make it as painless as we can. With cost-based pricing, you add up the costs of everything that goes into making your offerings (including your time) and add some profit to arrive at a price. To figure out how much you should add to your costs to establish your profit margin and selling price, look to your industry association to find out if there's a standard. But this is where most small businesses fail—they don't add enough profit because they don't account for the unexpected: having to fix a mistake, or not having time to pamper each and every client. And that's typically because they focus on having a competitive price with businesses that aren't even their competitors. They don't value their own input enough, or they have no idea how much profit they should make in order to be successful. While this model is a bit old school, it's a starting point for boutique businesses. This model at least ensures that you are making a minimum profit, but then you need to take it to the next step—demand-based pricing.

> "Competitive pricing can be effective for high-volume businesses that sell commodities. But you're not a high-volume business selling a commodity."

DEMAND-BASED PRICING: HOW **TO** SET YOUR PRICES

The theory of demand-based pricing is to set a price at what consumers will pay and then create the demand you need to meet that price. It starts with accounting for all of your costs like we did in cost-based pricing and then charging more. To succeed as a boutique business, you must have higher margins. You must then create demand. As a boutique business owner, you need to focus on creating demand based on desire for your products or services. The good news is that you don't do that by deep discounting. The challenge is that you have to get out there and make it happen. When you're creating demand, you can charge what you're worth every time.

Let's consider the classic lemonade stand as a simple example. Demand and prices can fluctuate based on the day's temperature—the hotter it gets outside, the higher you can potentially raise your prices because people will desire your product more. The hot temperatures just make people want it more. There are also other factors in establishing demand. There's availability—is there another option for a refreshing beverage nearby? And then, of course, there's the location—are you selling in a neighborhood where a $5 glass of lemonade is not too far out of the question? Or are you selling in a place where $0.25 is more likely to generate sales? All of these can influence demand for your product, and many times you have no control over these factors. However, in a boutique business model, you have to "create your own weather" and make people desire your product more. Even though you can't control how hot it is outside, you do have the power to create demand based on desire for your products. Maybe your lemonade is served over shaved ice. Maybe you notice that most of your neighbors mow their lawns on Saturdays, so you deliver your lemonade while they mow. Maybe you seek out the nearest walking trail and relocate your stand from a low-traffic neighborhood. Maybe you add to the experience of your stand by providing entertainment. The point is, you're creating more demand for your higher-priced products by using your strengths as a boutique business (we'll learn more about creating demand in chapter 11). Discounting businesses don't have the ability to copy that—they're too focused on volume.

> "In a boutique business model, you have to 'create your own weather' and make people desire your product more."

CREATING DEMAND TO SUPPORT YOUR BOUTIQUE PRICES

Here's the beauty of the boutique business model: you have the ability to create demand, which makes price much less relevant to the customer. Some boutique businesses establish prices using a little bit of all four of the strategies above. However, if you use a demand-based pricing strategy, you discover the highest acceptable price by creating the demand for yourself. Big-boxes and discounters can't do that. They create demand by using price discounts. They can't afford to create greater demand based on customized experiences. They can't sell their lemonade in hand-painted glasses or wash your car windows when you pull up to their stand. They don't have time to invite all the neighbors to socialize and share in a hand-mixed vodka and lemonade to discuss the Neighborhood Watch program. Nor do they even personally know their neighbors. As a boutique business, you can offer greater service, more customization, a better relationship, and more surprises. That's what creates your demand, and that's what you have the opportunity to do and—as a boutique that wants to charge "worth it" prices—you have the responsibility to do this. You can't sit and wait for the weather to change. You need to change it.

Another good example is the Neeley School of Business at Texas Christian University in Fort Worth, Texas. Dr. William Cron, associate dean of graduate programs and research, was challenged with the task of moving the relatively small MBA program into the most elite ranks. Competition was fierce, but the program couldn't attract top students and keep its strong reputation by competing on price. How could the Neeley School of Business set itself apart?

Dr. Cron took the initiative to shift the Neeley School's marketing efforts from a strategy based on affordability to one based on increased opportunity for the students. Dr. Cron realized that semester fees (vs. tuition) directly hit the Neeley School's budget and provided an opportunity to add much-needed services to the student experience, thus attracting upper-tier students. He proposed that the newly-afforded services would benefit students and eventually result in higher starting salaries upon graduation. With higher starting salary statistics for graduates, the school would attract a higher tier of student, who would also pay the higher semester fees. The additional budget provided the following services:

- **International Experiences**—there are six different international business trips students can take to study business in a market outside the United States, from South Africa to China. Students previously paid $1,750 for these trips in addition to their tuition and semester fees. Now this is included in the required semester fees. Prior to this change, only a few students took advantage of these opportunities because they had to pay out of pocket after they had already paid their semester tuition and fees. Now nearly 70 percent of the students benefit from the trips because the investment is included in the initial semester fee. This experience has driven up the starting salaries for graduates.

- **Employer Meet-and-Greets**—One week every semester, student organizations receive funding and a week off from classes to visit the nation's top employers in their area of study. A finance student may spend a week networking in New York City and learning at Goldman Sachs. Before the fee increase, these opportunities weren't available.

- **Specialized Career Placement**—Since the student fee increase, Career Services now has a budget to hire professionals working in specific career paths to consult students on how they can become more marketable to potential employers. These leaders share their networks, help with interviewing, and rework resumes.

> "People are willing to pay more when the product or service they receive is worth more."

Not only are the students thrilled, but the school also saw average starting salaries increase $20,000 and average incoming students' GMAT scores go up forty points, resulting in a more competitive applicant pool to choose from.

The point of all of this is simple. People are willing to pay more when the product or service they receive is worth more. It's all the extras you offer that create a demand for your product. It's the special way you serve your lemonade or the tangible results your students receive from an increased student fee.

CHAPTER 9 ACTION STEPS

1. *Find an accountant to teach you your costs of each sale. This includes the packaging, merchandise, and labor that goes into making your products or completing a service. This helps you to determine your bare minimum price (with no profit built in) and is KEY to understanding how to price for profit.*

2. *Research what amount of profit is characteristic of the best performing businesses in your industry. Back into your prices so that you can accomplish this desired profit margin.*

CHAPTER 10

The Scars of the Sale

A SIGN IN A DENTIST office declares "Any treatment—40 percent off regular price!" A local Realtor advertises lower commissions: Any house. Any price. Sound intriguing? Of course it does. We all like to save money. But, consider what a sale does to the value of your products and services.

Tanya worked nights serving tables at a franchise seafood restaurant. The job paid the bills. More importantly, the tips were enough for Tanya to save money while she studied to become a Pilates instructor. Because of the growing popularity of Pilates, it seemed to be the perfect time for Tanya to open her own studio.

Upon opening her doors, Tanya did everything a boutique business owner should do (including a lot of things you'll read about later in this book). She kept her job as a waitress. She was the queen of fitness during the day and slung king crab legs at night. She took the time to get to know her clients on a personal basis. She asked about their jobs, their families, and their health and fitness goals. She kept detailed information on each client so that she could provide phenomenal service and personalized instruction.

Years passed. Tanya's Pilates studio grew like wildfire. And before she realized what had happened, she had amassed a large following of Pilates fanatics.

Enter the competition—but only because Tanya made it her competition.

Approximately two miles from Tanya's small studio was a large gym. The club had always offered numerous classes to its members but had just announced a new Pilates class. Their classes were priced at less than a third of Tanya's prices.

Tanya heard from some of her clients that they were trying the new classes at the gym down the street. Of course, she got scared. She imagined all of her clients leaving for a lower price. She imagined herself going out of business—shutting the doors on her dream and going back to work at the seafood restaurant.

Tanya remembered the way her former employer would run price-driven promotions. She thought about the "all you can eat" deals and the oversized and over-discounted offers the restaurant chain would make to its customers. Tanya thought she should follow in those footsteps.

Instead of focusing on adding value to the relationships she already had with her customers by doing more for them, Tanya began competing with the gym down the street on price. In fact, she even beat their prices, doubled the number of classes she offered, and actually grew her client base by nearly 200 percent.

Now she felt like she was competing, but her profits were showing the opposite. And her loyal following wasn't as loyal anymore. The value of what Tanya offered them had decreased. They no longer received the personal attention, and because of the price cuts, most new customers were now focused only on getting the cheapest price.

Tanya's strategy had backfired massively.

With any sale, a boutique business owner risks devaluing his brand. A drop in price teaches the best customers to wait for a sale or consider other, cheaper offerings. And the scars of a sale can run much deeper. Consider what happens when designer jean companies create contracts for their once-boutique labels to be sold in wholesale discount clubs. Suddenly the product is no longer exclusive. It's not worth as much in anyone's eyes.

Sales seem like good ideas, but as a boutique, what questions are you planting in your customers' minds? Is it worth it?

> "A drop in price teaches the best customers to wait for a sale or consider other, cheaper offerings."

SALES ATTRACT PRICE-SENSITIVE BUYERS

Everyone wants a great price. But certain people shop specifically for the lowest price. They are less loyal. They don't care about the quality of what they are buying because nothing is more important to them than the price. You can't build the business you want with these clients. That's why it's important as a boutique business owner to ask yourself, *Who is my ideal client?* The client who values a high-priced luxury automobile may not value organic foods. The person who values racing bicycles may not value custom artwork. It's not about demographics (age, income, gender); it's about what is important to people. That's why we're not suggesting that you label customers by how much money you think they have to spend, but instead ask yourself, *What group of people loves what I do?* Do they want something you sell at a deep discount? Or do they really just want your product—a customized motorcycle, a homemade brownie with your secret ingredient, or a scarf hand knit with 100 percent wool in their favorite colors?

Academics confirm that deep discounting can tarnish a brand. Researchers from Harvard and Boston Universities took a deep look at the "daily deals" offered by Groupon and Living Social, including how those deals affect a company's rating on Yelp. Here's one of their conclusions: "We find a surge in reviews from new customers subsequent to the offer. But we also find that reviewers mentioning 'Groupons' and 'coupons' provide strikingly lower rating scores than those that do not, and these reviews reduce Yelp scores over time in our dataset." After a Groupon deal ran, they found that the average drop in ratings was 0.12. And if you think that's insignificant, the researchers also cite a study that found that for independent restaurants, a one-star increase in a Yelp rating leads to a 9 percent increase in revenue.[*]

One of our good photographer friends and her partner needed to generate more clients and were sold the promise of many new clients by a group-buying online discount service. They found several hundred people to take advantage of the deal they offered, but after two months of being beat up by discount-seeking clients who purchased the "deal," they began to think that their entire city was made up of bargain hungers who would spend the bare minimum. Our friend and her partner were considering restructuring their whole business based on these buyers who weren't even in their target audience. The scar of this one-time sale not only devalued their brand in the eyes of the loyal clients they had worked so hard to attract, but it also shook their confidence in a business model that had worked for them for ten years!

[*] "Daily Deals: Prediction, Social Diffusion, and Reputational Ramifications," arxiv.org/abs/1109.1530

DOES A SALE EVER MAKE SENSE?

While a sale attracts price-sensitive buyers, it also teaches your best clients to wait for a sale and devalues your brand over the long term. When you run a sale, you're sacrificing long-term profitability for short-term cash flow and attracting clients that will only buy when you have a sale. However, discounting can make sense in certain scenarios. Think of it this way: discounting products and services

> "Discounting products and services that you want to get full price for tomorrow doesn't make sense, unless you have a good reason."

that you want to get full price for tomorrow doesn't make sense, unless you have a good reason to discount price.

When you do discount based on the right reasons, you need to share those reasons with your customers. Here are a few scenarios in which discounting makes sense.

{Scenario #1}

FLEETING INVENTORY: If a hotel has ten empty rooms tonight, it can't sell those rooms once tomorrow hits. The revenue is forever lost. There are ways to sell that unsold inventory to last minute buyers at a discounted rate without cannibalizing full price sales and damaging your brand. People know that if they wait until the last minute, they may get what they want and they may not. To guarantee the hotel you want, you must plan in advance, and that guarantee is worth more. In a case where your business has fleeting inventory, this is an instance when you can safely discount.

BUNDLING: You may have some products that just naturally work well together, or you may find that your customers typically invest in more than one product or service with you. If that's the case, bundling may be a viable option for you. Insurance agents can often offer bundled packages to their customers at discounted prices. If you have your home, car, and life insurance policies with one company, you'll often see a discount on the overall rates over what you'd have paid if you had each policy with a different company. These bundles are discounted from the price of buying everything a la carte because the consumer is buying more. Consumers understand the reasoning behind bundling. They understand that they get a better price when they commit to spending a higher dollar amount. And, they understand that purchasing just one piece of the package will cost more if purchased separately.

{Scenario #3}

INVENTORY CLOSEOUT: Unlike most discounts, customers won't see discounts on almost-out-of-season products as a devaluation of your brand. Retailers must close out their inventory seasonally to make room for new products. Consumers get this. They understand that if they are the first one to purchase the latest fashion item at a boutique at the beginning of the season, they will pay a premium price for the privilege of having it first. And they understand that when they get a steep discount on the clearance rack at the end of the season, they're buying a less-valued item.

{Scenario #4}

PREPAYS: Prepays are the opposite of closeouts—customers get a better price for prepaying. They also understand that by prepaying, they've made a commitment to your company, and that's valuable to you. For example, if you pay upfront for ten teeth-whitening treatments at your specialty dentist office, you would receive a better price than if you bought them separately as you needed them. Also, as a business owner, consider that often things that are prepaid aren't ever redeemed.

{Scenario #5}

TRAINING: When you are training a new employee, it may be an opportunity to offer a limited-time special. This allows new clients who may not otherwise have come in to sample these services from the new employee. It also gives your new person experience. But keep in mind that when the prices go back up, you may not see those customers again. Try to offer this type of discount only to sporadic clients or prospects, not to loyal, long-time clients, so that you don't sacrifice profit from full-paying customers.

{Scenario #6}

SAMPLING: Suppose you own a nail salon and are offering a new product that lasts three times longer than a regular manicure. You overhear one of your clients talking about why she doesn't get manicures, just pedicures: her fingernails chip too much to justify a manicure. To incentivize her to become a manicure client, you may offer a discount on the new gel service, knowing that she will love it and return every three weeks to get her nails refreshed and maintained. (As a boutique, you might even consider doing it free one time.) This is different than sticking a "Half-off sale!" ad on your Facebook page, on a sign in your window, or in an email blast to your database; the one-time sample discount has context to the client.

{Scenario #7}

THE PARTNER DISCOUNT: The partner discount involves giving out free or discounted product to partner businesses that they can then pass on to their customers. Start by looking at your client list and identify other small business owners who share your same target market. For example, a photographer could give a stockbroker client with whom they have a great relationship a gift certificate for $200 to give to his most-valued clients as a gift. The stockbroker looks good for giving the gift, and his clients get artwork for their home. While the first $200 of photography is free to the stockbroker's client, his client will pay full price on the rest of his purchase. Really, everyone wins in this situation: the stockbroker's top clients believe that he purchased the full-price gift card for them, and the photographer gets a prequalified client who comes with a glowing endorsement from the stockbroker.

———

While I built my boutique photography business without discounting, there are times when it may be acceptable to have a sale, as long as it's within the parameters above. As you can see, the discounts discussed here aren't to attract new clients by throwing up a half-off sign because business is slow. However, it's important to determine how any sale might affect or devalue your brand.

Consider what happened with Tanya at her Pilates studio. It made her brand worth less. It made her product worth less. And it made Tanya's time and effort worth less. Bottom line on having a sale without communicating a good reason for it: if it has a strong chance of devaluing your brand, don't do it.

WHAT SHOULD YOU ABSOLUTELY, POSITIVELY, EVEN-IF-IT-SMELLS-LIKE-ROSES AVOID?

We know it's tempting to discount to generate short-term cash flow. We understand why offering a discount seems like a good thing. Yes, you could get a huge response from a sale, but then what? When you discount, you need volume to make up for the discounts. You're boutique, and you might not be able to handle that volume. Not to mention, when you discount, your customers begin to expect more discounts from you. But as a boutique business, you *don't* want your customers getting hooked on discounts. You want them hooked on you and the value you add to your products and services.

> "Bottom line on having a sale without communicating a good reason for it: if it has a strong chance of devaluing your brand, don't do it."

Sales can also change a client's perception of the value of products already purchased from you. Suddenly that $1,000 item they purchased at full price has a value of $750 now that you offered a 25 percent discount to their neighbor down the street. Here are the two types of discounts you should always avoid:

1. **Panic Sales:** Customers can smell desperation. A panic sale will not only devalue your brand, but it also typically

involves "emotional math"—the numbers don't allow you enough profit to continue operating your business the same way. You invest a lot of your time, creativity, passion, and hard costs into your business. Don't sell it short because you're having a bad day, week, or month. Just because a business is busy doesn't mean it's profitable.

2. Social Sales: Groupon and other online sites or group-buying memberships are great for driving customers to businesses. However, the sales they run are typically far too aggressive from a pricing standpoint for a boutique business to maintain that level of business. Plus, can you physically keep up with the demand from doing something that might turn out to generate a huge response? What happens to the value you add when your attention is divided between ten times your current number of clients? It suffers. And if and when you do draw in all of these new clients, you're instantly forced into making decisions based on the wrong target market— a price-sensitive target market. Not to mention, if you think you can convert a customer who paid $30 for your $115 product into a long-term customer, good luck. Customers will perceive the "social sale" price as what your product is worth, so next week when it's regular price, they will be unlikely to purchase.

> "When you discount, your customers begin to expect more discounts from you."

A sale can look like a great plan at first glance. You're thinking about bringing in new clients, creating revenue, and raising awareness for your brand. But it's important to understand that by discounting your prices, a sale also changes your brand. The perception of your company in your customers' minds will be different after the sale than it was before.

THE ALTERNATIVE TO DISCOUNTING— ADDING VALUE

We get it. There are times when you think the only way to attract clients or generate transactions is to offer a discount. But we challenge you to an alternative that is better than discounting—adding value to your existing offerings.

In your business, you can more readily attract the right clients by adding a value-added incentive when your clients make a purchase. For example, you might offer a free body-sloughing treatment when clients purchase a full day at the spa. You might also develop a loyalty program that gives your clients an incentive to return to you, maybe even more often than they typically would. This could be anything from a free gift with purchase to a special service to an extension of their service. This value-added strategy focuses on rewarding your clients when they spend more versus discounting the product before they've made an investment. By doing this, you keep your entire margin and you aren't devaluing your brand to your clients. They are motivated to purchase because of the extra incentive you are offering.

Take a look at the following example comparing straight discounting to a value-added incentive.

DISCOUNTING VERSUS ADDING VALUE: THE IMPACT TO YOUR BOTTOM LINE.

Strategy #1: Offering a 50 percent discount on a $500 product.	**Strategy #2:** Offering a product that retails for $250 as a bonus incentive for the purchase of a $500 product.
$500 Product	$500 Product
− $250 Less 50 percent discount you offered	− $ 75 Less your costs on the added-value item that retails for $250
− $150 Less your costs for the $500 product	− $150 Less your costs for the $500 product
$100 Profit	**$275 Profit**

In this example, you make nearly three times more profit by offering an added-value bonus versus discounting the original item.

When you use this strategy, you're attracting people who want something more and aren't just focused on price, just like a boutique business should.

CHAPTER 10 ACTION STEPS

1. Do you have any inventory that is fleeting?

2. Do you have any products and services that make sense to bundle?

3. Do you have times of the year when it makes sense to close out inventory? If yes, put it on your calendar.

4. Are there any offerings for which you can provide a prepay incentive?

5. Are you planning to hire a new employee? If so, can you offer an incentive to infrequent clients to get the new employee experience while they are training?

6. Do you have any new offerings that you could sample to a select group of current customers?

7. Think of the top five influencers in your community. The real movers and shakers who seem to know everyone who you'd like to be a client of your business. How can you incentivize them to talk about and endorse you?

8. Look through your database of relationships. Include people you already do business with as well as people you'd like to have a relationships with. Identify other small business owners with whom you can partner.

9. Brainstorm a few ways to add value to your products. How can you reward people for spending with you? When you're giving customers incentive to spend with you rather than creating orders by dropping prices, you're building your business the boutique way.

MARKETING & SELLING

As a boutique business owner, you charge higher prices. But that doesn't mean you should spend all of your budget on low-touch, mass advertising. TV, radio, and newspaper ads coupled with discounts is *not* the strategy that will create success for a boutique business. If you feel like you've tried everything to market your business and nothing has worked, this section will help you.

In the following chapters, we'll show you how to spread the word about your boutique business without using the same expensive tactics as the big guys. We'll show you how to create effective marketing pieces, how to build a dynamic database, and how to bring in business by becoming the go-to expert in your field.

And, yes, we'll have to talk about selling. But don't worry: boutique business owners never have to put on the hard sell. That's because marketing a boutique business is about relationships. Relationships with your clients. Relationships with other businesses. Relationships with charities. You need to be woven into your community— both in your industry and in your geographic location.

CHAPTER 11

The Boutique Marketing Difference

WHEN DR. RONNING OPENED HIS doors for business on day 1, he had the perfect concept—physician-supervised weight loss in a spa-like atmosphere. The facility was boutique in every way. Each customer would be greeted with a hot towel. They would sit in a leather massage chair while they waited to see the doctor, and would be offered healthy snacks like fresh fruit and nuts. All the while, a fountain trickled in the center of the room and soothing music played throughout. The only problem was that Dr. Ronning didn't yet have any customers to experience all the amenities.

Sharon opened her business the same day online. Her concept: home-baked cookies delivered in the mail. She had the perfect website—clean, appealing design with easy-to-order functionality. Sharon didn't have any customers yet either.

Both business owners engaged in some typical grassroots marketing—Dr. Ronning invited his network into the facility for a tour, while Sharon sent emails to her friends and family announcing her opening. Yet when it came to the core marketing efforts, they went in different directions.

Dr. Ronning rented a huge mailing list targeting his geographical area. He had twenty-thousand postcards printed. On each were a few bullet points that explained why his weight-loss system and facility were better than the competitors.

Sharon took a different approach. She made a list of all the local real estate offices. Then she started baking. Her marketing budget was spent on cookie ingredients and some really cool packaging—a box shaped like a house that had her logo printed on it. The box was fantastically designed to allow a waft of fresh cookie smell to sneak out of the chimney. It was impossible to ignore. Inside the box was an extra baggie of uncooked cookie dough that could be baked at one of the Realtor's upcoming open houses, since there's nothing more enticing than the smell of freshly baked cookies.

Sharon also included an engaging marketing piece that explained what she called "Connecting via Home-Baked Cookies"—her philosophy on why passing along something made from scratch can build an instant relationship. On the back of that piece was a short story, telling about how Sharon's grandfather baked cookies every Thursday afternoon for her when she was a child. He baked them all the way through her high school years. Even though grandpa wasn't the best communicator, he knew his granddaughter would sit at the kitchen table and connect with him for at least a few minutes while they enjoyed those delicious, warm, homemade cookies.

Sharon also made every attempt to get in front of groups to inspire them with her story. She offered to speak everywhere she could—not "selling," but sharing her story about how cookies resembled something bigger. She spoke to women's groups, networking groups, at luncheons and seminars. Everywhere Sharon went, she made new friends and added contacts to her list.

Dr. Ronning's twenty-thousand postcards were delivered. Sharon delivered forty-two cookie boxes and spoke at fourteen events. They both invested the same amount of money in their marketing approaches.

Sharon communicated her brand in high-touch, vivid detail that connected with her prospective customers on an emotional level. Her marketing materials were focused on building relationships. And she began growing her database, which is one of the biggest assets in your boutique business (more on that in a bit). Though both she and Dr. Ronning looked like boutique businesses from the outside, Sharon marketed like a true boutique business, using a high-touch strategy to attract the right clients one at a time.

THE MARKETING DISCONNECT

When you're boutique, your marketing efforts must be boutique as well. Boutique marketing is focused on reaching customers who aren't price sensitive, customers who want and appreciate all the extra things you do to make their lives better. Your marketing materials need to scream, "You're the most important part of our day!"

Discounters are focused on reaching large numbers of people who are motivated by low prices. The way they market can attract lots of customers. But it doesn't appeal to people who want the high-touch experiences we talked about in chapter 5. As a boutique business, if you try to attract people the way big-boxes and discounters do, you will attract the wrong type of customers.

Dr. Ronning might have come up with a great boutique concept and built a beautiful facility, but he didn't market like a boutique business. Postcards don't position him as different and won't get a great response unless they advertise a fantastic price. They are just too easy to ignore and throw away. By sending postcards, Dr. Ronning sent the wrong message to recipients: even though the images and wording on the postcards may have been perfect, a postcard by nature doesn't communicate that a business offers high-touch products and services. Dr. Ronning's postcards didn't show that he was dedicated to providing a more valuable experience.

Sharon, on the other hand, will attract the types of customers she wants because her marketing approach revealed her attention to detail, her commitment to spending time, and her eagerness to build a relationship instead of just making a sale. Consider your marketing pieces as a small sample of what you do, not as a message communicating what you do. We can't all make cookies to give as samples, but we must try to make a connection that gives people a true taste of our brands and the inspiration behind what we do.

BECOME AN EXPERT

Positioning yourself as an expert in your field is an inexpensive and powerful way to differentiate your marketing activities from those of the big discounters. What special expertise do you have in your craft, your products, your services, and your industry? More importantly, how do you convey that expertise?

By educating your customers.

For example, at Sarah Petty Photography, all of our artwork leaves archivally-framed. During the framing process, we educate our clients on the difference between rag mat and acid-free mat. I explain how there is actually acid in the center of "acid-free" mats and it will still eventually erode the artwork. Rag mat, on the other hand, is 100 percent cotton, and it will protect your artwork much better. Instantly, we've not only made our products and experiences worth our prices, but we've given the customer a new piece of knowledge that will help her make better decisions. It's the education that makes you the expert.

Scenario: Two different boutique lingerie shops open in your town.

The first shop is owned by Robin. Customers rave about the quality of her products—the finest silk undergarments you can find. Robin's shop is marketed and branded well. She has memorable advertising campaigns, including cleverly worded billboards positioned in the right neighborhoods. You are familiar with her brand, but you've never actually seen or met her.

> "Experts are people who educate."

The second shop is owned by Stella. Customers rave about her attentive service. She doesn't advertise much. However, you see her on television one day talking about how to choose garments that are most comfortable for your body type. Then you read an article in the newspaper geared at educating men on "foolproof gifts for Valentine's Day." And you hear her on your favorite radio station being interviewed about how to throw a lingerie shower for a friend who just got engaged.

Experts are people who educate, like Stella. They can often charge more. They're the people who get seen—those who are out in the world sharing the best ways to do this, fix that, prevent this, ensure that. Step up to the plate and show people what you know.

When you're the expert people want to receive advice from, they'll be willing to pay what your offerings are worth.

———

To succeed as a boutique business, it's imperative that you understand the differences between how you market and how the discounters market. Your focus is on getting in front of and wowing the right people, even if it's a small group. Unlike others, you're not going for the biggest reach possible. And you're further making yourself valuable by establishing yourself as the preeminent expert in your field. That's the boutique marketing difference.

CHAPTER 11 ACTION STEPS

1. *Make a list of things that make you an expert. What do you want to be the default resource for information on? Once you have a clear picture of the bounds of your expertise, make sure you know your topic like the back of your hand, and keep tabs on any current issues or debates going on.*

2. *Whether you're dealing with a client or presenting to an audience, interact like an educator. Take advantage of the fact that people love to learn. Look for opportunities to educate others instead of just selling them.*

3. *Become a media hound. Seek out media opportunities to educate the public and be viewed as the expert. Send press releases to local television programs explaining how you can educate their audiences. You want to be featured on television, on the radio, and in the* *newspaper—and you have to talk about more than just your latest product line or a closeout sale you're having. What media can you provide content to?*

4. *Make a beeline for online. An online following can create expert status overnight to the people that matter the most: your customers. Blogging, commenting on other blogs, and posting on social networks can quickly make you the expert in your customers' eyes if you give them advice that can improve their lives. What blogs can you comment on?*

5. *Seek out speaking opportunities. A true expert is frequently found in front of an audience. It doesn't have to be big. When I first started my photography studio I spoke to very intimate groups, like new moms' groups, to build connections and grow my business. When I founded The Joy of Marketing I started speaking at numerous photography conventions both large and small and now speak all over the world about marketing and branding. Speak to local groups or college kids taking classes on entrepreneurship. The more you speak, the closer you get to expert status. Where can you speak?*

CHAPTER 12

Building Your Database and Marketing Your Business

DID YOU EVER KEEP A little black book that held the names, vital stats, and contact information for all of your friends? Well, maybe those who were more than friends? In a boutique business, your database of customers serves the same purpose. It's not just a list showing you where everyone lives. Instead it details the likes and dislikes of a customer. How often do they purchase? How connected are they in the community? When should you call on them? It's your job to know the ins and outs of each customer. Your database is your business—it's the people who keep you in business. Without these people, you wouldn't be where you are.

The most important thing you can do as a boutique business owner is to build and nurture a database of people you have a relationship with. The discounters can't do that. Sure, they can collect their customers' demographic information, addresses, genders, and ages. But they can't pinpoint their personal lifestyles and buying habits. They don't know their clients' kids' names. Walmart doesn't know about the great portrait opportunity that came up when your baby lost his front tooth last week. It doesn't know that you have a passion for bicycling. It doesn't know that your parents' fiftieth wedding anniversary is next Wednesday. The big-boxes are way too big to have a personal relationship with customers. Other local businesses that are always discounting don't have the time to maintain relationships either.

This is one of your biggest advantages as a boutique business owner, but only if you capitalize on it. You must keep meticulous records of where your clients live, what they like to do in their free time, how often they come to you, how they first heard about you, where they work, and even the ages and names of their children and pets. The types of details you know about your friends are the types of details you want to know about your clients.

Your database is more than just a laundry list of names, addresses, and phone numbers. It paints an accurate picture of who your clients are. It helps you understand what you can do to earn their loyalty and repeat business. Each spring, at my photography studio, we go through our database to identify clients who have kids who are high-school juniors. We can quickly hop on Facebook to verify their grade level. We then send a personal note to these juniors telling them that we would love to take their senior portraits. A few days later, our phone is ringing. These are kids who have grown up coming to us and love us. This subtle reminder is all it takes to get our calendar full for the first month of the season. You can't possibly get this type of open-armed response with a cold, rented mailing list.

The sheer fact that it often costs ten times more to acquire a new client than it does to sell to an existing one is why it's so important for you to build that database and actively seek opportunities to add to it. It's tempting to think you can just run out and acquire a list of hot leads or new customers. But realize that your database is a collection of your relationships, and that it must be built carefully and over time. Your database must be filled with people who you know; some you may know well, others you may have just crossed paths with, and some you know of and would like to know better.

Your focus should be on constantly prospecting different places to add people to your database. It truly is like a little black book—it holds current relationships, past relationships, and potential relationships. Think about your database in personal terms. If you were looking for a date to your best friend's wedding, what would work better: randomly calling people from the phone book, or focusing on your little black book of friends and acquaintances?

> "Your database must be filled with people who you already know; some you may know well, others you may have just crossed paths with, and some you know of and would like to know better."

Where can you go to add people to your database? And who should you be adding? To increase your likelihood of success in turning prospects into customers, you want to start with people you know. Just like in the wedding-date scenario, you have a better chance of getting a sale if you've had previous experience with a client, regardless of the capacity. It doesn't matter if you originally met a potential client when you were working at a past job and are now a business owner; that prospect knows the quality of your work and your personality and is more likely to use you for his needs rather than a stranger.

If you are a boutique business, the size of your database is not nearly as important as the quality of customers within it. Yet we see it all the time—companies assuming that acquiring tons of leads improves their marketing prowess. They don't give thought to how valuable the names on the list are. The relationship with the people in your database is what insulates you from the competition.

HOW TO BUILD YOUR LITTLE BLACK BOOK AND YOUR BUSINESS AT THE SAME TIME

Depending on the nature of your business, you'll discover that some of these ideas will work better for you than others. However, we suggest giving them all a try, and keeping an open mind to new ways of expanding your database. The key is to take it one name at a time, and make each name count. You can't afford to pass up opportunities just because you may only get ten leads. One of those ten might become your biggest and best customer, supporter, or evangelist.

1. Network. Networking doesn't just mean going to an event to shake hands and exchange business cards with everyone you meet. Instead, it means being connected with a specific group of potential customers. It means finding the right places to network, and working with others who are trying to reach the same networks as you. Most boutique business owners can share stories about being "at the right place at the right time" and meeting a great customer or partner. But don't sit around waiting for serendipity—the reality is, relationship-builders put themselves in the right places.

2. Volunteer. By volunteering, you are demonstrating your commitment to your community and showcasing your skill set to others who share your values. Look at volunteering as an opportunity to gain exposure for your personal brand and build relationships with people you can add to your database. Early in my tenure as a business owner, I volunteered to sit on the board for a local juried art fair. As an owner of a creative business, I knew that my fellow volunteers were also people who valued art and could potentially become clients. And, of course, I am passionate about art. While I didn't aggressively seek new clients during my volunteer tenure, my skills as a professional photographer did come up

> "Great networkers put themselves in the right places."

in conversation a lot. I made many new connections, and I saw so many of my clients at the annual event. Volunteering for something my clients and I were both passionate about helped position me as a leader in the community and helped me build relationships with others who value the same things as me.

3. Offer a "freemium" on your website. Because you're an expert at what you do, you have knowledge to share with others. For example, a fitness trainer could offer the top five exercises for creating sleeveless dress–worthy arms. When you raise your hand to indicate you want an illustrated PDF that demonstrates the movements, you're asked for your email address so they can stay in touch with you and keep providing you with more exercise information.

4. Incorporate charitable marketing into your business.
Cause-based business-building activities are great places to meet people who will want to support you because you both support the same cause. The best part is that people who make donations to charities are generally prequalified because they are non-price-sensitive buyers. If they have money to donate to a charity, they more than likely have disposable income to invest with you. A few years ago, at Sarah Petty Photography, we teamed up with the Ronald McDonald House for a charitable marketing promotion. During the month, all session fees generated from the Ronald McDonald House's donor list were donated back to the charity. To let people know about the promotion, Ronald McDonald House mailed a sponsored marketing piece to thousands of people in their database. You can see the piece online at www.wortheverypennybook.com/charitablemarketing. By teaming up with this organization, we were giving new but like-minded people a reason to invest in photography and benefit a great cause. We walked away with many new relationships, many leads, and a great feeling of accomplishment. Some of the clients that came to us for the first time as a result of our promotion with Ronald McDonald House are now among our best clients. In this instance we didn't generate any publicity, but most of the time we benefit from quite a bit of media attention from fund-raising efforts. In this economy especially, a business helping a charitable cause is often deemed a newsworthy event.

On a smaller scale, auctions are another way to promote your business while helping a nonprofit or school. We recommend donating a product or service to a silent or live auction rather than a drawing or raffle. This way, you know that the buyer is someone who is interested enough in your product to pay something for it and hasn't just been chosen randomly. Remember, as a boutique business, you aren't all things to all people and you don't necessarily want a gift certificate in the hands of those who don't value what you do. Sometimes the auction will provide you with a list of those who bid on your donation so you can follow up with the non-winners, too. Even if it's a small list, these are people who have raised their hand and shown an active interest in what you do, and they should definitely be in your database.

5. Initiate co-marketing partnerships. No matter what you sell, there are other businesses reaching out to the exact same clients that you want to reach. No, they aren't your competitors. Instead, they are the wine to your cheese. Both of you attract clients who appreciate and value the same things, people who have the same sensibilities. Co-marketing with these businesses can grow your database quickly. But co-marketing isn't just list-swapping; it's getting warm introductions to the customers of other businesses that you admire and that share your ideal prospective customer. And it's also making introductions between your current clients and your co-marketing partners.

To find potential partners, first look at who is spending money with you. Do they have a database? Stockbrokers, insurance agents, mortgage brokers, personal trainers, luggage store retailers, private clubs—they all have relationships with people with disposable income. Start by thinking about how you can help them build their businesses. Then you can think about how they can help you build yours. We've found that by first giving to others and helping businesses grow, many doors will open for you. You'll also want to look for co-marketing partners who legitimately love what you do. You want someone who will naturally gush about you to others, not someone who feels like they have to carry out their end of a business deal.

So what do actual co-marketing activities look like? It could be a customer-appreciation event, a fund-raising event, a mention in your newsletter, or even a direct promotion—telling your customers about other resources they might be interested in exploring. The example we talked about in chapter 10—giving a gift certificate to the stockbroker to re-gift to his own clients—is another good example of co-marketing. Even if you get only three new clients, those clients are already emotionally engaged with you and are enormously valuable because they were introduced to you by someone they respect. Because you want that respect to be passed on, you must choose your co-marketing partners wisely. They need to be organizations you actually would use and in many instances already *do* recommend to your customers.

6. Host an event. Hosting or co-hosting an event is a fabulous way to attract new clients. For example, a photographer might team up with a veterinarian to host an event at the new vet clinic. She might invite the local boutique groomer, the pet bakery, the doggy day care, and the dog-training company to join the co-marketing event. The photographer might set up an area to take photos of each owner and his or her pet. The groomer might give trims. The baker might give a doggy bag of organic pet treats, and the training company might teach the dogs a new trick each hour. Everyone invites all of the people in their database. Everyone shares in the costs. We aren't talking about a trade-show type sales situation, but rather an environment created full of fun, sampling, and education for the people who attend. Every business that attends has the opportunity to collect names and build their databases. All attendees could be given a gift certificate for a free bag of organic doggy biscuits when they sign up for training. Or they could get a free grooming when they purchase a pet-and-family photo package. If the event is a success, the businesses could even continue to work together in the future. This is a qualified and engaged audience that will turn into a base of new clients for all of the businesses involved. Before you host an event, check out the top twelve things that are critical to hosting an event at www.wortheverypennybook.com/event.

7. Speak. Yes, we talked about it in the last chapter—the value of public speaking, and how it establishes you as an expert. But, since we know a lot of you are terrified of public speaking and may have pushed it to the end of your list, we thought we'd bring it up again with the addition of another benefit—it's an amazing database-builder. When you speak to educate your audience, your audience begins to develop feelings of trust. And once they've met you and experienced your expertise, people will want to continue connecting with you. Teaching people something they don't know makes them want to know more about your business and how you can help each other. It doesn't even need to be speaking on a big stage. Host a workshop. Invite your client to bring her mommy group in for an afternoon informal educational presentation. Again, your focus is not to sell, it's to teach and build deeper relationships and rapport. A chef might hold a workshop on how to cook gluten free, or how to grocery shop for a child with food allergies. A real estate agent may host an event on how to stage your home for a quicker sale.

The goal is to create an opportunity to bring the people to you and let them experience your expertise.

8. Rent a list. A list you compile yourself will always generate a better response than a cold list you rent. But there may be times when you need to rent a mailing list. If you are brand new in a community, have no clients, and don't know anyone, the fastest way to build a database is to rent a list of people whom you consider your ideal client and send them a gorgeous establishing piece via the mail like Sharon the cookie baker did in chapter 11. Or suppose you want to test interest in several different markets. You might do a sample mailing to rented lists in three or four different cities to see which group of customers is most likely to make the drive to your location. Or maybe you've expanded your services into a new segment of people. Suppose you have a window-washing business and most of your clientele is residential. But recently you purchased a large crane to be able to reach very tall buildings. You might rent a list of business owners in your city who own commercial property to create a demand more quickly. The bottom line with lists is that they are a starting point, not the final answer.

DEATH BY POSTCARD

Many business owners try to connect with their databases by sending out a postcard. It's cheap and it's quick. But the thing is, everyone does that. Go check your mailbox. Then check your recycling bin. You see lots of postcards in both places, right? The postcard is dead because everyone does it. In fact, it died a long time ago, and your business is as good as gone if you think a plain old postcard is going to result in customers pouring through your door. So, if you're building a high-end business, why would you misrepresent yourself by sending a low-quality marketing piece?

People see postcards as junk mail. They position you as a lesser-value, lower-priced company that doesn't understand its audience. It's the equivalent of spam in your email inbox. It's amazing how many business owners will say they've "never" responded to junk mail but still want to spend their marketing budget on a postcard.

If you were a high-end chef, would you let people sample foods that don't represent the true quality of your food? Of course not. You want people sampling your best. So if you are building a high end business, why would you misrepresent yourself by sampling a low quality marketing piece?

How do you overcome the "junk mail syndrome"? Don't create junk.

In many industries, business owners can buy postcard templates and simply slap on a logo and contact information. It's inexpensive. It's easy. It's plug-and-play. The imagery and photographs on the postcard are generic. There's nothing personal about it. Everyone in your industry is doing the same thing. These cards make a beeline to the recycling bin.

> "How do you overcome the 'junk mail syndrome'? Don't create junk."

On the flip side, remember the piece we mentioned earlier, the one sent out to introduce Sarah Petty Photography? It was a piece that cost several dollars per mailing due to the quality of card-stock and the die cuts. But given the response, it was worth every penny. It paid for itself many times over with just one new client.

Your marketing piece doesn't have to be uber-expensive, but it does have to show your investment in getting the attention of a new client. As a boutique business, one right client can make a huge impact on your business. Here's an example we love.

Aaron, a landscaper and palm tree specialist in California, wrote handwritten letters to customers in the neighborhoods he wanted to service. He explained in the letter that he understood there were a lot of options to choose from, but that none of the other options would offer his attention to detail. Aaron also made sure to mention a specific tree, shrub, or structure on the recipient's property so they would know that each letter was personalized.

Aaron showed his potential customers that he was serious about caring for their lawn—he didn't just tell them, as most businesses would've done. He showed he wanted each customer's business by investing his time in analyzing their lawn before he wrote the note.

The point is, your business is boutique. Therefore, if you're going to approach potential customers through the mail (which we highly recommend due to your ability to target customers), you've got to send something that separates you from all the other businesses out there. If you want to be seen as different, you have to do something different. Think quality rather than quantity. Your marketing piece needs to be amazing—it needs to actually interest the recipient. It should let potential customers get a taste of your dedication. It should demonstrate that you've taken the time to truly research your clients' needs.

Is there a right time to send a postcard? Yes, there are times when you might need to send postcards—but there are still better ways to get people's attention. Sending postcards might be an effective strategy for time-sensitive messages like clearances or a mailing-list cleanup. If your products are discounted for clearance, it might make sense to contact your audience with a lesser-value marketing piece. Just be sure that your postcard is not your first touch point with potential customers.

YOUR ESTABLISHING PIECE: A POSTCARD ALTERNATIVE

Remember that brand standards manual we talked about in chapter 2? Much of the image you've established will appear in your marketing materials—your logo, fonts, colors, taglines, etc. And we suggest using your standards manual to create one (yes, we said just one) marketing piece that becomes the "This is who we are" establishing piece. We would rather you use your budget to create that one wow piece than waste funds on a sad little template postcard or other mass advertising effort. When you can afford to do a second activity really well, then add that.

Of course, you might notice that we're not using the word *brochure*, and that's for good reason. What do you think of when you hear the word *brochure?* Probably a tri-fold little thingy that has a few pictures and lots of unnecessary words, right? It includes a lot of stuffy info about how and when a company was formed and a lot of *blah blah blah*. Our advice is to save that stuff for the secondary navigation on your website. The analytical buyer may want that information, but it doesn't need to be in your establishing piece. The goal of this piece is to create something that evokes emotion and makes people want to know more about you and your business. You want this piece to generate leads, make the phone ring, position you as a leader, and encourage prospects to refer you.

Instead of a borefest of a brochure, create an establishing piece that shows what you do, and make it your intent to recreate in the recipient the same *emotion* (that's the word you need to remember) a customer feels when she does business with you.

Be a control freak with your establishing piece. Think of it as that one great picture you use everywhere online, on all your favorite social networks—your go-to profile picture. Your establishing piece is the one thing you want to share with everyone.

How do you do that? Remember these simple rules.

1. Quality is a reflection of quality. All of your marketing pieces—but especially this one—must mirror the quality you offer to your customers. If you received a beautiful marketing piece from a company and showed up at its retail location or online store to find something completely opposite, you'd be irritated and disappointed and wouldn't trust the business. The same is true in reverse. If you sell quality, you need marketing pieces that mirror that quality. There is no magic answer to how to convey the quality you offer, but if you can create a piece that folds, twists, or sings when people interact with your marketing, it will help generate the response you want.

2. Most people don't read, they look at pictures. Your establishing piece has a split second to grab someone's attention and pique their curiosity. So keep the written part short. Instead of massive content, shoot for massive emotion and focus on tapping one of the five senses. If you're a restaurant, make them salivate. If you're a designer-clothing shop, think about how your message tweaks their self-perception. Be wary of too much content.

3. Emulate other's results, not other's brands. You're marketing your brand, not your competitor's. So often boutique business owners will attempt to emulate someone in the same industry or business, copying them almost exactly. But how will you ever stand out if you're doing the same thing as everyone else? Get creative with your establishing piece and make sure it markets only you. Of course, you can look at trying to emulate the results of successful companies and people. But realize that Disney became Disney because it was a leader—it set the bar. And that company you view as the one to catch up with? As soon as you copy it, it will come up with something new—it was creativity that made it the leader of the pack.

4. Hire a pro—someone who wants you to be different. Would you let an amateur represent you when your life is on the line? Of course not. So when your business is on the line, hire a reputable graphic designer and reputable copywriter for your establishing piece. Often, you can work cost-effectively with these fellow creatives by trading goods and/or services. You offer something cool and unique—how could it benefit them? A photographer could offer to trade a photo shoot for a designer's next campaign. A web designer might offer to build a website for a copywriter in exchange for some web content. Think of how you can create a mutually beneficial relationship between you and the professionals who work on your big marketing piece.

With a professional, attention-grabbing establishing piece, you have a powerful tool you can use to drum up business and expand your database for months if not years.

CHAPTER 12 ACTION STEPS

1. Buy database software. Find a program that will help you categorize and sort your customers in the most ways possible. An inexpensive version from your office store will work just fine.

2. If you haven't already, set aside some time to make a list of all your current contacts, friends, and family members. It doesn't matter if they're not your ideal customer—you never know who they might know.

3. As you add more names to your database, make a point to collect as much information as you can: names, addresses, family info, how they came to you or how you know them, career, type of buyer, where their kids go to school, pets, type of car, interests, affinities, charities and clubs they participate in, etc.

4. What networking opportunities exist in your community? Get involved and plan to attend one per month.

5. Name two places you can volunteer where your clients also volunteer. Reach out and see how you can help.

6. What can you create to give away on your website that will excite your clients and help build your database with the right buyers? This should be educational, not a coupon.

7. Find a local charity that is excited about working with you. Make sure it's a charity supported by members of your ideal client base. How can you help them reach their goals?

8. Identify other businesses that share your prospective ideal client and reach out and offer to help them. Build a relationship with businesses that you can help and that can help you, too.

9. *Can you engage with other business owners to co-host an event? Or can you excite your existing clients by hosting an event that they'd love to attend? Events give you an opportunity to check in with your clients and give them a little more love without having to ask for a sale.*

CHAPTER 13

The Lowdown on Low-Touch Advertising Options

THAT LITTLE GEICO GECKO IS adorable. We've seen him a billion times. We laugh at his snarky little comments and his cute little body. He's extremely likeable. He's attention-grabbing. And we recognize him immediately.

Guess what? He's worth millions. And as a boutique business, you'll never be able to afford him as a spokesperson. He took millions to create—millions of dollars and millions of impressions.

Consider this. There are gobs of marketers out there spewing out rules of thumb about converting someone into a customer. They'll say things like, "A person needs to receive your marketing message three times before they acknowledge your existence." And then they'll say, "Once they acknowledge your existence, it takes another four to seven impressions before they understand your offer." That may be true for many types of small businesses—but not for boutique businesses.

Your goal as a boutique business owner is to create opportunities for high-touch marketing—again, it's a trade-off between quality verses quantity. When prospects receive that high-touch piece, it moves the right kind of buyer to action.

Some people say that direct mail is dead. We totally disagree. People love to receive mail (unless it's a bill). It's up to you to make it worth their time to read it. The only people who think that direct mail is dead are the people who aren't sending or receiving cool, interactive, eye-catching pieces. And that's true for all of your marketing activities. They need to be high-quality. They need to be high-touch. And they need to be unmatched in their coolness factor.

Let's compare a few different types of marketing tools. Some reach numerous people, and some are more high-touch. All of these options can enhance your current strategy, but they have to be run through your personal boutique filter. Are the messages and advertisements you use created with the highest quality? How do they reflect your brand? Do they communicate the value you offer to your clients? To attract the high-quality clients you want, show the high-touch, high-quality experience you offer through your marketing materials, regardless of the vehicle you choose to use to deliver them. Here are some traditional advertising and marketing activities and our take on them.

BROADCAST MEDIA: It's called "broadcast" media for a reason—the audience is typically broad. Can you afford to spend money trying to attract people who would never be interested in your product? No! However, if you truly feel that radio and television advertising is necessary for your business's success, focus your budget on highly targeted audiences. For example: a specialty kitchen store might run ads on the Food Network. Or a high-end clothing retailer might run a heavy advertising schedule during celebrity entertainment news shows where fashion is often a hot topic. It's still not high-touch like we prefer, but if you're dead-set on investing in broadcast media, at least make sure the audience is extremely niche. And the biggest thing to keep in mind is that if you're going to run TV ads as a boutique business, they must be high-quality production. They need to be of the same caliber as your business—and that will take a chunk of your marketing dollars.

NEWSPAPER: Instead of buying an advertisement in a big newspaper, consider writing an educational article that could be featured in small local papers or local lifestyle magazines. Reach out to the lifestyle editors of these publications—they're always looking for great content. Keep in mind that this shouldn't be confused with an advertorial—a copy-heavy paid piece cleverly disguised to look like editorial. Make sure your pitch is educational to the reader, and get rid of anything salesy. If you're a photographer, you could pitch an article about how to get great newborn photos at the hospital. If you own a high-end home audio company, you could pitch an article about how to arrange your furniture for better acoustics. The point is, the content of your article has to benefit readers. Make sure you understand who the publication's reader is.

SALES LETTERS: Which are you more likely to read: a mass-produced, laser-printed letter, or a short, handwritten, personal letter? Sales letters can be effective marketing tools, but they're also tricky. Realize that most sales letters, no matter how well they're written, immediately communicate to the recipient that they're one of the many receiving the letter. Plus, they typically include a special offer—which is great but leads back to a discounting strategy. Writing a good sales letter is an art form. If you're going to do it, hire a pro, and be sure that the letter is filtered through your boutique brand. At the end of the day we suggest using other marketing routes, simply because sales letters are so difficult to perfect with a boutique brand.

EMAILS: Oh, there are so many emails in all of our inboxes each day. And so many are deleted without being read. Think about the emails you get from companies you do business with. What do they say? What makes you open a message? Your emails must contain valuable information; otherwise recipients will stop opening them. An orthodontist may email a list of candy that is "braces safe" just before Halloween. A neighborhood auto repair facility could send an email explaining how to winterize your car. The point is, the messages you send to your customers need to be interesting and helpful. They need to show that you've invested time in sending useful information.

But no matter how great your emails are, always make it easy for recipients to opt out.

ONLINE OR PRINTED NEWSLETTERS: A regular newsletter is a good way to reach your clients, whether you email them or send them in the mail—and it's usually free or inexpensive. The key is to be consistent and pack the newsletter full of useful information for the reader. Sadly, we see newsletters fail all the time. A company will start a newsletter and then not keep it up; the newsletter will be so random in its timing that it confuses the customers; the content will be boring or generic, or all about the company, not the reader. Figure out the seasonality in your business and correlate your newsletters to that cycle. When do your customers care the most about your business? That's when you want to approach them.

Our final word of caution: be very careful if you believe that email and online newsletter marketing is your best option because it's free. You should only reach out using this tool if you have valuable information to give your clients. Email marketing should supplement your other, higher-touch marketing efforts. Free marketing tools shouldn't be your only marketing efforts. Because everyone else is doing them, it's very hard to distinguish your boutique business using these tools alone. And be sure to keep a super-watchful eye for errors, misspellings, and typos that might turn off your customers. One tiny mistake and suddenly your free advertising can cost you a lot.

TELEPHONE: First, cold-calling rarely works for boutique businesses—we're all bombarded with telemarketing calls, and we've all grown callused to cold-callers. Nevertheless, *warm*-calling current customers can be effective as long as the call provides concrete benefit. For example, "Hello, Mr. Jones, I'm calling from Marie's Bakery and wanted to let you know that we now sell pumpkin bread for $12.99. Could I reserve one for you?" isn't cold, but it does scream, "Just buy more!" Instead, try this: "Hello, Mr. Jones, I haven't seen you in a while and I noticed that your wife's birthday is coming up at the end of the month. I thought I'd reach out to see if you'll be ordering a cake again this year. Is there anything special I could do for you?"

ONLINE: It wasn't too long ago that an online presence was just an option—bricks and mortar were the true test of a business's respectability. But all that has changed. Today, you must have a strong online presence or you're perceived as behind the times. Your website must communicate your brand appropriately. It needs to showcase your identity, and it needs to function properly. It needs to emulate the experience your customers would have with you in person in your retail location (if you have one) as closely as possible. Consider your website just as important as giving a potential customer a tour of your business. What do they see? What do they hear? How do you give them a sample of your product, service, or experience through your website?

This is why we recommend investing in a professional web designer and using the best tools for your online shopping cart. One company we like is Shopify.com, which specializes in giving boutique online retailers an attractive and functional online shopping cart. They know that for boutique businesses, the design and the user experience must be better. With a better site, the boutique online retailer appears more reputable and trustworthy, which creates a stronger brand and takes the emphasis off price. And even if you don't have a budget for a top-of-the-line video shoot that represents the experience your customers get with you in person, there are incredible cost-effective tools. One of our favorites is Animoto, which helps you use images and music to create a professional video presentation of your business. Your website should sing your brand. Invest in it just like you would invest in making your brick-and-mortar experience the best it can be. And don't even think about skimping on the photography. If you've put your heart and soul into building your brand—choosing the right products, investing in the most gorgeous packaging—but you display poor-quality photos on your site, you'll devalue everything you've worked so hard to build.

———

If you have the impulse to buy up prime broadcast or print ad space and send out mailers galore to promote your business, it's time to rethink your marketing. What works for the big guys doesn't work for you. They can get away with low-touch initiatives, automated and mass distributed. You, on the other hand, need targeted, personal, engaging content that reaches the right people, even if it's a relatively small group that receives it.

CHAPTER 13 ACTION STEPS

1. *Take a look at everything you're doing to market your business. How many low-touch activities are you doing? Is there a way to put your boutique spin on them?*

2. *Create a marketing and publicity plan and set a timeline to achieve each item on your list. Maybe it's blogging once a week. Maybe it's sending out one press release a month. Or maybe it's committing to three speaking engagements a year. Put your plan in writing, and let someone you trust hold you accountable for it. A profitable boutique business isn't reactive. They plan proactive marketing strategies to attract the right buyer.*

CHAPTER 14

Nurturing and Rewarding Your Best Clients

MEET LIZ. SHE OWNS A catering business that specializes in kosher foods. One of her clients, the Berksons, are a family across town that has hired her for numerous events—birthday parties, graduations, anniversaries, and two weddings. The parties are typically not too large, but the setting is always a lot of fun. Liz gets excited about their jobs. And, the family has introduced Liz to many other customers who host similar gatherings.

Another client of Liz's, a financial investment firm, hires her to handle the catering for all of their business events. The firm hosts educational and promotional seminars to the public. The events are huge, but the environment is stiff. The organizer is often sharp with his words. The requested menu doesn't make Liz excited to get into the kitchen. And as far as Liz is aware, the firm has never recommended another client to her.

Liz knows that her business has grown dramatically because of the Berksons. They have kept her pipeline full with new clients, which makes them more valuable to her business. So should Liz treat them differently?

YOUR BEST CUSTOMERS: THE 80-20 RULE

By categorizing all your clients, you'll quickly be able to decipher who the best ones are—the 20 percent that have earned more of your attention.

Enter the Pareto principle, more commonly known as the 80-20 rule. Basically, the 80-20 rule says that roughly 80 percent of effects come from 20 percent of the causes. The rule gets its name from an Italian economist, Vilfredo Pareto, who studied income and wealth distribution and found that a large percentage of wealth was held by a small percentage of people. Over the years, this economic theory has been effectively applied to everything in life from pea pod yield to the clothes we wear. Think about it, you probably wear 20 percent of the clothes in your closet 80 percent of the time. However, what makes the Pareto principle really interesting is how it applies to all businesses—about 80 percent of your business will be driven by 20 percent of your customers. The rule can be held up against numerous things in life, and it proves to be fairly accurate. So what's the point? You can't be all things to all people. You know that 80 percent of your business is driven by 20 percent of your clients, and this gives you an advantage—if you focus on treating the top 20 percent of your clients better, you can expend less effort and reap fantastic rewards.

As a boutique business, you don't need to sell to everyone. You offer second-to-none products that consistently thrill your customers. You offer a service-focused relationship that makes your customers love you. And, as a boutique business, you have the opportunity to pinpoint your top 20 percent—the customers that drive your business—and give them a reason to brag about you. It's simple. Find your best customers, treat them like gold, and you've found a strategy that leads to customer loyalty and mega-success.

Consider what The Wardrobe, a women's upscale clothing store in Springfield, Illinois, did for its best clients. Many years ago, the owner of The Wardrobe invited the store's best customers to her lake home for a sneak preview fashion show. The weather was perfect, and drinks and appetizers were served. And because the owner's home is shaped like a U, it served as the perfect location for a runway, where these top customers got to model their favorite attire from the store. Not only did this make the best clients feel extra special; it engaged them with the small business owner and her staff. And engagement is hard to come by in an oversaturated market.

> "If you focus on treating the top 20 percent of your clients better, you can expend less effort and reap fantastic rewards."

Or consider what Jobing.com, an Arizona-based Internet job board, did for its best customers. When Jobing.com was launching a massive new blog, they asked their best customers to become bloggers—sharing advice on how to write better resumes, improve their interviewing skills, and dress for success. By featuring these top clients, it gives them the opportunity to connect with more potential applicants and gain a reputation as an employer of choice.

Rahr and Sons Brewing, in Ft. Worth, Texas, engages its best customers by inviting them to the brewery to be a part of helping with the bottling process for a day. Fritz, the owner, not only likes to hang out with his best customers; he also wants them to feel like they're members of the Rahr family and experience firsthand how amazing it is to be a part of this process. After the bottling is done, he orders pizza for everyone who helped.

Your best customers deserve to be treated better than the average Joe. Invite them to special events, create special opportunities that the public doesn't have—anything to show them that they're valued. If you do it well, they'll come back again and again, and sing your praises freely.

DELIGHTING YOUR TOP 20 PERCENT

What do you do to delight your best customers? How do you make sure that your business continues to grow from the clients you want to do the most business with? Clients who love you become your soldiers, your evangelists, your fans, and your supporters. It's not just a great marketing strategy; it's your job to take care of the 20 percent of people who drive 80 percent of your business. Here are some ways to do that:

"Your best customers deserve to be treated better."

1. Reward your favorites. Your favorite clients should be the first to hear about special opportunities, closeouts, new products, and exclusive events. Maybe you're an antique shop that wants to clear an area of the store to showcase new items you acquired at an auction. You might open an hour early for your best clients to give them first dibs on new merchandise. A real estate agent might treat her best clients differently by revealing hot properties to them before the listings get pumped out to all the newspapers. An online niche, custom-made skateboard shop might offer limited-edition boards signed by a famous skater to its best customers. People feel great because it makes them feel extra-special.

Give your best customers first, last, or extended opportunities to further engage with your company. It's okay to treat customers differently. Clients are not your children, so you don't have to love them equally. It's also okay to let the world know that you treat your best clients better. In the big-box space, airlines and hotels do this all the time by offering perks like special privileges, amenities, and services to the customers who spend the most. However, for boutique businesses, these rewards are more critical—you don't have the massive numbers of best customers huge corporations have. In fact, you only have a few, so you must take the absolute best care of them.

2. Educate your favorites. Customers like to understand the how and why of the products and services they buy. If you're an interior design firm, treat your best clients to a free class on color and texture. If you're a wardrobe consultant who just became privy to the hottest new designs in Europe, offer a "Before the Runway" webinar with your favorite clients. If you build custom motorcycles, invite your customers in to watch a bike get detailed. Constantly brainstorm new ways to bring your top 20 percent into the process for a behind-the-scenes look at what you do.

3. Cut the strings. While you're rewarding, educating, and connecting with your top clients, there doesn't need to be strings attached. We've all been to the events with the high-pressure sales pitch at the end. We've been to the "educational opportunities" that force you to write down the names and contact numbers of five family members or friends. When pampering your top 20 percent, there are no strings—you're giving something away without expecting something in return. It's part of your brand, and people will trust and refer you more when you delight your clients without strings attached.

4. "Fire" undesirable clients. It's tough to push a less-than-favorable but high-profit customer off to the side. Yet, if you want to create your dream business, you've got to do it. Some clients can suck away your time, your energy, and your passion for what you do—leaving you too depleted to give fantastic service to your top clients. At first, you may not have to "fire" an undesirable client. They may demand less of your attention if you stop giving it all to them. They may end up realizing that you're not at their beck and call and leave on their own. But if they don't get the hint, you may have to let them go. These discussions aren't pretty, however, we recommend softened honesty rather than passive-aggression. Often the most difficult customers are the most price-sensitive customers, which makes us really lucky as boutique business owners—our prices typically filter our customers for us.

DIVIDE AND CONQUER

When you know every person in your database intimately, your job as a marketer becomes pretty darn easy. But the question we always get asked is: How do I categorize the people in my database? Our answer: *As many ways as you can.* Your database can be divided into current customers, prospects, and past clients. It can be divided by age group, buying trends, life circumstances—the list goes on, right down to each individual as an individual. The point is, the more you know, the more personalized your communication can be. And the more personalized your communication is, the stronger your relationship will be with each customer.

Your Customers: Who are They?

Here are five categories we use to help us better understand the needs of all the clients in our database.

1. The Big Fish: These are the people who love to spend money with you. They're the people who truly seem as if they can't buy enough of your stuff. But, realize they're coming to you because they love you, and you need to love them in return. When you establish great customer relationships, it doesn't mean you should offer discounts. Clients who are willing to dig deep in their pockets are typically spending big because they love and trust you. Take exceptional care of them, and they will take care of you.

2. The Steady Eddies: Every business has a few loyal fans who return over and over again. It may be because they love your business, or it may be because they're creatures of habit. Consistent customers—the Steady Eddies—offer extreme value even if they don't spend the most money with you. The key is to discover why they're hooked on your business and look for opportunities to give them more. Help these people stay on pattern. If a customer typically comes in every six months and hasn't been in for ten months, reach out to them. They'll love the reminder!

3. The Matchmakers: There are some people in life who are simply connectors. Some connectors may spend very little with you and visit infrequently—in fact, you may hardly consider them customers at all. But they might be connected to the leaders of all the big fund-raising events, other vendors who would make great partners, or other people who could help drive your business. These infrequent but well-connected customers are the Matchmakers. Matchmakers may even bring you referrals without ever purchasing from you. At Sarah Petty Photography, we had a Matchmaker who was so in love with our photography that she referred oodles of new clients to us. The irony was that this woman didn't have children of her own and had never experienced the studio as an actual client. Your job is to gush over these people and show your appreciation often. Also, reach out and share new ideas so they can keep playing Matchmaker.

4. The Choir: These are the customers who will sing your business's name from high atop the mountain even if no one is listening. These customers may be big spenders or little spenders. They may visit frequently or infrequently. But they're sure to talk about you with glowing regard at every opportunity. They are your fans, your evangelists, and some of your biggest supporters, and what they tell the world about you is invaluable. One of my favorite clients, Jennifer Mogren, set up a fantastic display of my work on easels outside her office (she was the elementary school nurse) to brag about how much she loved the images of her children. She is definitely a soloist in our Choir. I didn't even know she was doing this and heard about it through the grapevine. When it comes to having an evangelist, it doesn't get better than that—someone bragging on you because they love you and your business so much. Because we want to reward our Choir members and keep them singing, we are always looking for special ways to appreciate them. If we are creating a gorgeous promotional piece or hanging a new display at a prominent location in town or need models, we look to our Choir.

5. The Taste Testers: This group presents a huge opportunity even if it's not made up of your best customers. The Taste Testers are the customers who will try you out on a small scale. They'll watch. They'll observe. And they may even go to your competition for a taste. They are, however, a powerful group once you harness their loyalty. Why? Because they're the thinkers—they weigh every option before making a commitment. This is your opportunity to give these people the amount of time and attention they really want—the kind they probably won't get from someone else. It's your opportunity to give them the education they seek to make their decision. It's your opportunity to blow their minds with follow-up services, erasing any lingering doubts about price-shopping. Taste Testers will present all their research to their friends, families, and networks. They'll tell everyone about the time you invested with them and everything they learned from you, and they may even join the Choir.

USE SOCIAL MEDIA TO CONNECT WITH YOUR DATABASE

When you're building out your social networks, you need to actually become friends with the people on your database rather than seeing them as channels to sell to. We're talking about befriending them, treating them the way they've shown they want to be treated, and engaging them the way they've shown they want to be engaged. If you a see client in the newspaper because her son was given a scholarship, send a personal note. If you are friends with members of your database on Facebook, LinkedIn, or any other network, and you see that they posted something interesting, comment on it. We once saw that one of our clients was running a school fund-raiser, and because we were listening, we had the opportunity to reach out and donate a studio gift certificate for the auction. The goal is to become more of a friend than a service provider. It's all about building and maintaining genuine relationships.

Social media is a hotspot for boutique business. And it's a great way to nurture your database—but only if you do it right. Social media is not a place to post your rapid-fire sale (which you won't do after reading this book anyway) or push your products every hour. Your database will turn you off if you invade their social space with sales messages. However, they'll be turned on by your approach if you treat them like friends. Listen, share, and connect with all the people in your database if they'll allow it and as long as you don't overstep their boundaries. Would the clients of a boutique salon be interested in watching a new product demonstration on how to straighten curly hair? Sure. But do they want to hear "Call me today for a consultation" over and over and over? Not so much. They want information they believe they won't get anywhere else.

HOW TO GENERATE REFERRALS

First of all, if you're not receiving at least some unsolicited referrals to your business, then there's something wrong. In this case, go back to your core identity, your style, the "wow factor" that makes you different. Something needs to be fixed before you do any more marketing. When you're delighting your customers by truly running everything you do through the boutique business model filter, you should be naturally generating referrals. And because you are so spectacular, it should be easy to ask for more referrals.

Yes, even though you should be getting unsolicited referrals, you still need to ask. Look for opportunities to plant the referral seed before you do business by telling the client that you want to give them the highest level of service so the entire transaction will be worthy of their referral. Then, look for opportunities to ask for referrals when your clients are gushing over you. Asking while they're enamored with you not only positions them to gush about you to others, but it also reiterates the value you gave the client—it reminds them that your business is definitely worth it. However, this process just doesn't end with getting customer referrals. Ask your vendors, partners, and others in your community for referrals. Ask businesses you co-marketed with to give you referrals. Reach into the organizations and businesses that know you and know how great you are. Wedding photographers should be talking to the church wedding coordinators. Flower shops should be reaching out to dress and tuxedo shops. Be generous in singing the praises of other organizations. Set that tone. Tell them that you've referred them, and they'll be excited to refer you. And finally, pay attention to how people are already referring you to others. What aspect of your business are they gushing about? Listen carefully. That feedback will tell you where to direct your attention.

A DATABASE-NURTURING STRATEGY

There's nothing more frightening than when a family member is sick—especially when that family member can't tell you how they feel. In this case, the family member is a Yorkshire terrier named Sydney—a sweat pea.

Sydney's temperament was typically spirited and energetic. But suddenly the family noticed that something was wrong. Sydney was sick.

Sydney's family called the groomer to cancel an appointment they had that day. But knowing how great a fresh haircut can make anyone feel, the groomer offered to come to Sydney's home.

That type of above-and-beyond action is what we call a "random act of love"—and every boutique business must find new and surprising ways to deliver them to customers.

Consider what Creech Plumbing in Weatherford, Texas, does for its clients. It's a family owned and operated business that spreads plenty of love to its clients and receives oodles of love in return. When the price of stamps goes up, Creech Plumbing sends its clients an envelope of one-cent stamps—in essence making its clients' lives better and solving other problems for them, even if the plumbing is in tip-top shape. And when clients do have a plumbing problem (usually the least-favorite home repair issue) and call Creech Plumbing, they're sure to always get a handwritten thank-you note from Mrs. Creech.

Random act of love? You better believe it. Creech Plumbing is the hero in the situation, and *you* get the handwritten thank-you note! Whether you have one customer or many, if you create random acts of love from the start, you'll create goodwill, generate referrals, and solidify lifelong clients who love you.

Random acts of love, and the strategic thinking behind them, give you the opportunity to surprise and delight your customers. These little actions have a huge impact. Random acts of love show your clients that you're paying attention to their needs. They show that your boutique business and your brand is worth the price— and that your relationship is worth maintaining.

NOT-SO-RANDOM IDEAS

Below, we've compiled a list of random acts of love that you can apply to your business, simple ideas that you can use—perhaps with some tweaking and honing—to show love to your clients and nurture your database. And, although we've categorized them by industry or business type, plenty of them can be employed by everyone. Maybe they'll even prompt you to think of a better idea on your own.

RETAIL/SPECIALTY: A keepsake shop owner might hear from a customer that his daughter is moving away to college. A random act of love would be to send a goody bag (chocolate chip cookies, an iTunes gift card, and a framed picture of the family) to the student. But what kind of goody bag can you send off to really ease the anxiety? A special bag that goes to Mom. Or, better yet, Dad (who's probably not showing his emotion about the change as much).

FOOD/RESTAURANT: When you see your best clients walk through the door, let them skip the wait in the lobby. Ask them if they'd like a complimentary sample of a new wine you carry. Give them the bottle on the house and ask them to share their thoughts. Erin recently made reservations at Wink, in Austin, Texas, for her husband's birthday. There was a large group of friends celebrating, and because the restaurant is one of those tiny little places where the chef is always in the kitchen, she was worried about getting a big enough table. Well, Wink went far beyond the call of duty. Erin's party arrived that evening to find that the restaurant had printed happy birthday wishes to her husband on that night's menu. At the end of the night, they gave them a menu, signed by the chef, to take home to forever remember the evening. Erin is still talking about it. She has recommended Wink to many friends since then.

ART/CREATIVE: Gobs of opportunities exist for creative businesses. A graphic designer we work with, Katie Loerts, created customized note cards for each of us. She burned the designs onto a disk so we could print them off whenever we chose. We loved it. She showed us how talented she was and surprised us in the process.

A copywriter friend of ours had a client who was getting married. He wrote a poem for the couple and had it printed on top of a photo of the couple that his wife had taken at their engagement party. The image was printed in black and white and then digitally lightened so the poem would be easily read. Then the copywriter had the image framed and wrapped as a gift. The couple loved it so much that they not only had the image enlarged so that they could display it at the reception, but they also used it as an invitation to a five-year anniversary party. And, today, it hangs in their home.

REAL ESTATE: Realtors get an inside glimpse into how people feel about certain types of architecture. If you have a client that loves Frank Lloyd Wright's style, send him a coffee-table book of photographs of Wright's work.

FITNESS/EXERCISE: A personal trainer might show up at the finish line of a customer's first half-marathon with a big sign showing support. Or she might bring a sack of post-race necessities like Advil, ice, and a cold beer. Or she could drop by her client's office with a rich chocolaty protein shake, especially if he admitted to having afternoon cravings for sweets. Or she could give a client who just reached a weight-loss goal a gift certificate to a boutique jean shop or bathing suit store.

CLOTHING: If you're paying attention, there are a billion ways to throw out random acts of love when it comes to clothing. Suppose one of your best customers comes in and purchases one of your most expensive dresses and a few days later you get a new shipment of merchandise with a bracelet that complements the dress perfectly. Stick it in the mail with a thoughtful note. What a great surprise.

HAIR/NAIL SALONS AND SPAS: The owner of a boutique nail salon might notice a client's post on Facebook about how she spent the entire day doing laundry and washing dishes. The salon owner might then send a quick message encouraging her to stop by the next day for a complimentary touch up of sealant. The owner of a spa might overhear a client talking about his upcoming vacation to the beach and send him a huge sun hat.

ONLINE BUSINESS: When you're an online business, you have to work harder. Random upgrades to free shipping, personal notes or calls, sample packets, etc., will go a long way in showing love. One of my favorite skincare companies surprises me from time to time with travel-size samples of new products when they ship my order.

ANY BUSINESS: It doesn't matter what type of business you operate—these next little random acts are winners every time. Nominate your customer for a prize or mention their name in your blog. Ask them if they want to be a model in your next advertisement, or ask them for a testimonial ("because you're my favorite"). That's showing appreciation and giving them a little fame. That's being a friend. And it's a winner every time.

—

CHAPTER 14 ACTION STEPS

1. *Identify the most fruitful ways to segment your database. Start by breaking your customer list down by demographics, psychographics, and lifestyle segments.*

2. *Make a list of your very best clients—the handful of people who are your biggest fans. Identify one way to reward them as soon as possible.*

3. *Make a list of your worst clients—the ones who leech away your time and energy and do little but foster negativity. Effective immediately, put them at the bottom of your priority list.*

4. *In the coming week, share at least three random acts of love with your existing clients. Don't go for the expected. Really shock someone by going out of your way for them.*

5. *Find clients you haven't seen in a while. Go to social media to see what they are up to. See how you can create random love.*

CHAPTER 15

How to Sell Boutique

SELLING: IT'S THE WORD THAT makes so many business owners, especially in the boutique world, cringe. It conjures up this
terrible feeling of pressure, schmoozing, and manipulation.

That's really not good selling, and definitely not a boutique
business version of selling.

We understand why the word *selling* has such a negative con-
notation. It's because, as consumers, we've all been that person
who has felt pressured to buy. We've heard the strong-arm pitches.
We've heard the "Buy now and save!" mantras. We've heard the
"Nobody beats our prices!" rantings. We've heard the scripted
cold-calls. These are the classic tactics of discounters, who try to
cast a wide net and bring the sales home by pressuring people.
They live by the philosophy that one person can convince another
person to buy a product because the price is too good to resist and
the timing is too perfect to walk away.

When you're boutique, you're not about pressure. You're about going out of your way to organically attract customers who appreciate what you do. Many discounters don't actively badger consumers to buy from them, but they use rock-bottom prices to try to force sales. Compare a mass retailer like Hobby Lobby to a niche frame shop where the owner knows everything about every frame. You may not get the bargain prices at the boutique store, but you will get a person who goes out of her way to explain and educate you on the framing process—not to mention a customized frame.

Or consider a medical spa that offers Botox injections. You can get them everywhere nowadays. One spa will sell to you on price—telling you that you won't find a better deal in town. When you agree, she sticks the needle in you and sends you on your way. It might not have been too high-pressure, but it definitely wasn't high-touch. She didn't educate you on your skin type or let you sample some products she thought might be helpful to your skin. She didn't try to create a relationship with you in any way, shape, or form. She didn't give you any reason to recommend the service to your friends. Nothing about the experience surprised you, delighted you, or brought you joy—and you won't even remember the place. The only thing you'll remember is the price.

Down the street, you find another medical spa selling Botox injections. When you inquire, the representative doesn't tell you that it's the lowest price in town. Instead, she tells you that you should first find out whether Botox is really the thing you need. Then, she uses state-of-the-art machines to analyze your skin and wrinkles. She shows you images of your skin and where you might have potential problem areas. She shares options with you and gives you ideas on how to prevent further aging, which will actually save you money on Botox over the course of your life. She offers to give you a sample of a new cream and finds out when you would like her to reach out to schedule your next Botox appointment.

And she asks questions and keeps a profile form so that every time you come, she instantly connects with you and can find solutions to problems you didn't even know you had. As the expert, that's what she should be doing for you! That's selling boutique style.

I was teaching a workshop a few years ago to clients of The Joy of Marketing. We had covered a good portion of what you're reading about in this book—how to market as a boutique business, brand, price, create a unique product mix, and experience. We had taken a break during the workshop, and when we returned, I said that we were going to tackle selling. One woman dramatically dropped her head to the table in front of her—obviously I had struck a nerve so powerful that she didn't even want to look at me. When asked, she told me that she hated making people "buy things that they didn't want." That's *not* what boutique selling is.

Selling as a boutique business is the opposite. Your job is to create demand for your offerings by sharing the benefits to your clients and prospects. You won't have a business if you don't sell. However, as a boutique business, your job is to find out how your offerings fill your clients' needs and point out the solutions you offer. You have the advantage of knowing those needs because you have a close relationship with your clients. When you create a demand, you aren't making people buy things they don't want, you are making them want the things you are offering. It's your job to solve problems in their lives. Listen to them. Develop rapport. Help them discover their needs. Because you're a helper and not a typical salesperson, boutique selling should be an enjoyable, rewarding process.

The Blues Jean Bar in Santa Monica, California, creates sales by delighting customers when they step up to the "bar" and ask for their desired brand, style, wash, and size of jean. Sure, consumers could get the exact same pair of jeans elsewhere, but it's the Blues Jean Bar's expertise in finding the perfect fit that keeps customers clamoring for more. And, customers also rave about the service—touting that once you enter a dressing room, the "jean-tenders" won't stop serving until you've found the perfect jean to match your lifestyle. Ask anyone. The perfect fit is priceless. When you don't get that level of service, you end up rifling through racks trying to find the right color, fit, wash, size, and style. A basic description like "boot cut" doesn't help you if you're concerned about having a little more junk in the trunk, or if you're really tall, short, or curvy. The Blues Jean Bar gets it. They look at your body type, notice your style, ask several important questions about your likes and dislikes, and make immediate recommendations to please you. They create sales the boutique way: through amazing service and a process that thrills customers naturally. No pressure necessary.

YOU AND YOUR TEAM MUST BE ABLE TO SELL

It's time to change your perception of selling, and it's important that your team changes its perception of selling as well. We want you to embrace selling in a new way.

Here's the core difference between discount selling and boutique selling.

- **DISCOUNT SELLING:** The sales process involves little or no engagement between buyer and seller. Discounters focus on selling large quantities of products to price-driven buyers. No one holds the buyer's hand. The relationship between buyer and seller is based on the discount. Because the sale is transaction based, after the sale, the relationship is over.

- **BOUTIQUE SELLING:** There's high engagement between buyer and seller. You build rapport, you get to know the customer, you spend time educating them. Your first thought should be, *What problem do they have? How can I help them?* You get to know details of their life and you take detailed notes. And because the sales process is relationship based, the service and experience continue after the sale (for example, the boutique stereo store might come to your home and make sure the installation works properly, training you on how to use all of the pieces that were just installed).

- **NO-MAN'S-LAND SELLING:** This is where you are not a big box, yet you are not acting like a boutique. You don't have the volume to get the margins without selling like discounters. You don't have the time to get sales like boutique businesses. This is the worst place to be.

SELLING SKILLS ARE MORE IMPORTANT IN THE BOUTIQUE MODEL

The difference between your sales process and the sales process of discounters is night and day. However, that doesn't mean you don't have to be as good at closing the sale. In fact, you have to be *better* at closing the sale, but in a different way. You're not doing it by adding pressure. You're not negotiating on price.

You close sales the opposite way. You close sales by doing so many things to please the client from the first interaction to the last that the phrase *close the sale* doesn't even come to your mind. You close sales by educating clients, viewing them as friends, looking out for them, and paying attention to their individual desires, needs, and concerns. You close sales by giving them over-the-top service and an experience they can tell their friends about. You help them discover their needs by becoming their friend and asking all the right questions. Yes, you have to sell, but instead of giving the smooth-talking sales pitch, you're searching for solutions that will absolutely, positively satisfy their need and bring them joy.

Consider the cosmetic dentist who specializes in porcelain veneers—you know, those spectacular teeth that all the movie stars have. Veneers are now becoming common in dentistry—so much so that you can find discount dentists offering the service. But think about it. Are you going to get permanent fixtures in your mouth because there's a guy selling them for cheap? Or are you going choose the dentist who goes to dental conventions twice a year and writes articles educating others in the industry about new techniques for installing veneers correctly? We would hope that if your smile is a priority, you're going to choose the one who approaches the process carefully—making sure the new veneers will work properly in your mouth. The one who ensures that you get the perfect color—nice and white, without turning your mouth into a flashlight.

For the sales process to work, it's the relationship you build in the sales process that means so much to your customers. And you have to be active and aggressive not about closing the sale but rather about adding value and joy to their lives throughout that sales process. You have to actively sell. You can't just take orders or wait for customers. You don't have the luxury of droves of price-motivated customers showing up at your doorstep to grab products off your SALE shelves. For this reason, you need to give attention to the ones you do have.

To get started on the path to mastering boutique selling, follow these five rules.

1. Overcome price objections in the first conversation by focusing on benefits. Price becomes a major issue only in the absence of value. Make sure that, in your first connection, you build value through education. At Sarah Petty Photography, many people ask about digital files and prices. But we know that before a customer can possibly make a decision on price, they need to know what makes our studio different. In the first conversation, we must build rapport by asking many questions about their needs. We tell customers why our business is different and how everything we do benefits them. We educate them on why we only use high-end materials, even though it requires more time, work, and attention. We then share prices. By then, they know if we are the right photographer for them and price is no longer and issue.

2. Be confident in your prices and your value. Much of the perceived value you create with customers is in presenting your prices in a positive way. It may take some practice if you're just starting out, but much like dating or interviewing for a job, your demeanor with clients has to be nothing less than confident. Don't apologize for your prices.

3. Be willing to walk away from a client. It's a hard lesson to learn, but when you spend time on the wrong clients, they wear you down and make you lose your passion. And, worse, you start making decisions on price and service based on the wrong buyer! We see this all the time when boutique businesses sell via Groupon or other coupon services. All of a

"When you spend time on the wrong clients, they wear you down and make you lose your passion. And, worse, you start making decisions on price and service based on the wrong buyer!"

sudden, you have swarms of new, price-sensitive clients vying for attention and service. The next thing you know, you're making business decisions based on the needs of the wrong customers. Your brand suffers. The relationships you have with your current customers suffer. The level of service you provide sinks into something sub-par, but you're too exhausted to think about marketing to the right people.

4. Don't wait for the phone to ring to sell. Because you have relationships with your clients, you can go *create* the sales when times are slow. You have the advantage of creating demand by selling to your current customers, co-marketing with other businesses, or working with a charity to add new clients to your database. Have an event. Go out there, get the right clients, and create something magical for them.

5. Be honest. As a boutique business, you have to have a strong moral compass so that you will always be able to do what's right. If something goes wrong, you need to do the right thing to remedy the situation. That means you have to have margins that allow you to do the right thing—always. This is especially critical to understand during the sales process. It's why we tell people that negotiating on price is not good for business. If you agree to a lesser price and find yourself in a situation where you need to do the right thing, you won't be able to afford it.

———

We completely understand that a lot of people—especially those who are driven to start a boutique business—aren't comfortable with the idea of selling. Fortunately, closing sales as a boutique business owner doesn't involve pressuring customers or adopting a cheesy persona. You just have to be you. Build the relationships, learn about your customers, understand their problems, and you are on the right path to generating sales.

CHAPTER 15 ACTION STEPS

1. Make a list of the most common objections you hear in your business. What benefits can you share with your clients to overcome each objection?

2. List all the benefits of your products. What's in it for your client if they invest in you?

3. Practice saying your prices in a positive way while conducting mock sales. Add a video camera to really challenge yourself. In this case, perfect practice makes perfect.

4. Make a list of rapport-building questions you can ask your clients to help identify their needs.

CHAPTER 16

Rules to Live by as a Boutique Business Owner

Before we wrap things up, we want to give you some quick and dirty rules to live by as you build your boutique business. To stay on top, your business has to grow and mature; it has to remain consistent and reliable while constantly surprising customers and surpassing their expectations. That doesn't mean you need to focus on franchising, add a ton of overhead, and become a big discounter yourself. It doesn't even mean you have to expand your client base. But you do need to stay vigilant, exercise sound judgments, and grow as a business. Here are a few rules to help you along the way.

1. Find the next level and move up. If you're going to grow, you can't be content with the same old products and services. You always need to be looking for the next level. You need to be scrounging for the next product, treatment, service, application, or trend. You always need to be thinking about the next way you can wow your customers. You can't always bring the same bag of tricks. Successful boutique businesses have the latest and greatest.

Set goals for launching new and exciting products. You may not know what the next best thing is yet, but if you set dates for when you want to launch the next best thing, you'll hold yourself accountable for finding it. Go to industry conventions. Look at other industries. Read magazines. Always have your idea radar turned all the way up. You never know where the next big idea will come from (and no, it shouldn't come from your competitor).

2. Stay hyper-focused. Successful boutique businesses don't assume they can be all things to all people and are at ease saying they're not the right fit for some. Your job is to grow—your customer base, your product line, your level of service, and your quality levels—within a very narrow focus.

Ask yourself three simple questions when considering any idea.

- **Does it fit my brand?** For example: Does placing an ad in a shopper magazine compliment my brand or hinder it?

- **Does the idea help my business grow, or does it just spread me thinner?** For example: Does adding twelve new products actually increase my profitability, or will it decrease my productivity? Will it confuse the heck out of my customers?

- **Does it allow me to maintain my profit margins?** For example: Will growth increase my overhead costs? Or will a new, lesser product cannibalize my current product's value?

3. Prepare for risk. As a boutique business, you only play to be the best. And that takes some calculated risks. Your customers expect you to try the extraordinary. They want you to discover or invent the newest, coolest, hardest-to-find, and most-difficult-to-copy items and services. Risk can be your friend. And you have to understand when to take them to win.

For example: Let's say you're considering buying a new building or retail space. To justify the risk, you need to check your financial statements and ensure that your business can sustain the growth. We don't recommend leaping into a risk based on hopes and dreams. If your business today can support the growth—the new building, the new technology, the warehouse space—go for it. But if you're just crossing your fingers, hoping that the risk will produce more business, see if you can create more business before taking the leap.

Ask yourself these questions when you think a growth strategy is risky.

- **How much will it cost if it flops?** For example: If a risk requires you to carry a large inventory, add extreme overhead, or change your current mode of operation, it should be carefully considered, and you should have an idea of how much it will cost if you fail.

- **How valuable is it to promote yourself as an early adopter?** Will this risk enhance your image as an early adopter, and will customers appreciate that? If your customers view you as someone who offers the best products and service, then they expect you to take risks and will probably support you through a few ideas, products, and services that don't fly as long as it doesn't change your brand.

- **Is it consistent with my brand?** Are you the rogue copywriter who submits risqué material to magazines or pushes the envelope with advertising messages? Or are you the sensible jeweler who only buys the absolute highest quality and stands behind everything you sell? Some risks can be weighed when you consider whether they're consistent with your image and reputation. Your brand will lead you in the right direction. Follow it.

- **Will my customers love it?** Taking risks for any other reason than delighting your customers is the riskiest business of them all. If your customer won't love a new product but you're getting a hot deal from a manufacturer, then you're doing yourself a huge injustice. Take risks when your customer will love you for it, and avoid risks for any other reason.

4. Find a mentor. There is wisdom out there that you can posses today simply by reaching for it (and investing in it). Look for the people who successfully do what you want to do and who have used your business model to get where you want to be. We are both MBAs and we still invest tens of thousands of dollars each year in business education. It might seem like a steep cost in the beginning, but education from people who have been there, done it, and are succeeding will accelerate your business growth faster than any other activity. Education needs to be part of your budget. Don't sell yourself short by skimping on learning opportunities. Other people just like you have spent their entire careers figuring out the secrets to mastery. Connect with them. Learn from them. You have the chance to shorten the learning curve.

5. Grow toward the light. Learn from your houseplants. They grow toward sunlight because the sun keeps them alive. Your customers are your sunlight. Grow toward them. One of our favorite authors, marketing guru Seth Godin, teaches that businesses should grow by creating products for their customers, as well as customers for their products. Grow by growing your relationships with the people who already know you, love you, trust you, and pay you.

Pay attention to the things your customers love, and try to find ways to copy that success in a new way, with a new product, or with a new service. You know everyone in your database. You know your customers' buying preferences. You know their likes and dislikes. Study those areas to find out how you can grow toward the light—by giving your customers more of what they want instead of focusing all of your efforts on trying to bring new customers into your family.

> "It might seem like a steep cost in the beginning, but education from people who have been there, done it, and are succeeding will accelerate your business growth faster than any other activity."

As the years pass and your business matures, revisit these rules regularly. While consistency is important, stagnation and complacency will eventually result in bored and restless customers. Harness the fun of owning a boutique business by constantly looking for new sources of inspiration and new ways to grow, learn, and educate.

CHAPTER 16 ACTION STEPS

1. *Find a mentor—someone whose business is where you want yours to be. Attend a workshop. Buy their educational product. Seek out more from them.*

2. *Spend time brainstorming some new products and/or services that you can offer next year. Make it a goal to roll out at least two new offerings in the upcoming year.*

3. *Make a commitment to ongoing education. Commit a budget and invest in you! Get it on the calendar now. Don't wait until you have time.*

CONCLUSION

You CAN Be
Worth Every Penny

IT WAS APRIL FOOL'S DAY, 1974. That day, in Tempe, Arizona, a pipe dream was born for Tom Brodersen, Gayle Shanks, and Bob Sommer.

Just kids at the time, these three entrepreneurs envisioned a socially responsible community meeting-place. So, with $500, a stellar deal on a bookstore that was considering closing its doors, and a goal to remain focused on serving the community, they embarked on a journey that many of you reading this book have also pursued—launching, living, and maintaining a profitable boutique business. The result was their business: Changing Hands Bookstore.

What does "boutique" really mean? You know the answer to that now.

Pop in at Changing Hands Bookstore to see how its owners define *boutique*. On any given night, you might happen to catch a book signing by people like bestselling author Stephenie Meyer of the *Twilight* series, rock star Ozzy Osbourne, Secretary of State Hillary Clinton, or comedian Chelsea Handler, or you may happen upon a group of local poets mesmerizing an audience with thick prose.

Yes, at Changing Hands you'll find the latest and greatest bestsellers—the books you can buy at any big-box or through the Internet. But right down the aisle you might find locally made chocolate toffee. And on another aisle you might find specialty gift items—things you really can't find anywhere else. Along with the hand-picked local products that sit side-by-side with national bestsellers, customers at Changing Hands find what they can't get most other places: an intelligent, well-read, and friendly staff eager to hand-sell books to readers young and old. Better than a cursory Amazon search, the booksellers at Changing Hands talk to customers every day and help them find new ideas, new thrills, and new inspiration in the pages of their many titles. Trained to serve and excited to fit readers with the right books, the staff is what really keeps customers coming back. It's a custom experience that perpetuates the brand that the store's owners developed back in the 1970s.

What a great example of a boutique. Changing Hands has a strong connection to its clients. It brings together a group of people and makes them a part of a community. They don't succeed by having the lowest price. The boutique mentality permeates the way its owners think, behave, interact, and dream for the future.

BEING BOUTIQUE: BUY THE WAY YOU SELL

Money can often be touchy topic. And, as you read through this book you might have felt uncomfortable a time or two as you wondered whether you could truly operate beyond discounts and whether your customers would agree with your decision to be profitable. We understand. But before we set you free into the world with a big to-do list, here are some final thoughts about being boutique.

When you're a boutique business, you can't just sell as a boutique—you have to buy as a boutique. That might sound strange at first glance; however, think about how buying from boutique vendors elevates your products and services. Think about how buying boutique instantly builds you a network of support. You're creating relationships with other people who conduct business like you do (and who probably share customers with you). Think about how you can weave yourself into the fabric of your community and build connections with the business owners who are concerned about your city, community, and neighborhood. Think about how buying boutique integrates you into the boutique community—where co-marketing can happen in an instant and where relationships grow over a handshake between business owners. When you're boutique, buying boutique brings huge advantages.

Take us, for example. Yes, we're passionate about boutique business models. We're passionate about finding them, talking about them, and sharing great practices with the world. But we're also passionate about giving our business to them. The publisher of this book, Greenleaf Book Group, is a great final example. No, they're not the biggest publisher. In fact, the truth is the opposite. We could have gone to a big-box publisher. But we wanted someone to hold our hand through the entire process. We wanted someone to steer us in the right direction while allowing us to have input on every step of the process. From the fonts, to the design, the paper, and the cover stock, we needed a publisher that understood how important all of these details were to our message. And, that's exactly what Greenleaf provided—a process and learning experience tailored to our needs, and a book that delivers our message. Was it a larger investment for us? Absolutely. And it has been worth every penny.

IN CONCLUSION

Is your identity the face you want to show customers? What are you doing to make it easy for people to fall in love with your brand? Are your offerings worth what you charge? Are your experiences worth more? Does your marketing mirror your brand? And, are your prices worth it to you and your customers? Answer all of these questions. If there are still disconnects, then you have some work to do or a decision to make. We're not saying that you have to use the boutique business model. If you'd rather compete on price, that's ok—but you just read the wrong book. However, if you want to be a business that delivers on your passion and doesn't compete on price, then the boutique model may be for you.

Remember, being boutique is different. You're boutique because *you* are the heart, the brain, the hands, and the joy behind the value you create for your customers and the profits you create for yourself.

EPILOGUE

For Those Who Haven't Done It Yet

CUBICLES CAN FEEL LIKE PRISON, and we know that many of you, as you've read this book, have wondered whether it's time to free yourself from office incarceration. You'd rather dive nose-first into your passion—working for yourself, snapping photos, teaching fitness, creating artistic pieces, or searching for the next really-super-cool-but-impossible-to-find product. Who wouldn't?

Sandy hated her cubicle. Her day job was as a data-entry manager at an insurance company. It wasn't a great fit for a creative person like Sandy, but it paid the bills. Nevertheless, she would have rather been chasing her passion—sewing at home or running a shop selling her own products. The question was, would she ever find that freedom?

Backtrack to a day at the pool. Sandy's son was taking swimming lessons. The kids were all in the pool, and when the clock hit the top of the hour, they all came dashing out to find their towels. This is where Sandy identified a problem, and an opportunity. Near the boys' changing rooms hung eleven beach towels. Three were abstract and beach-themed. Three were towels she had seen at Costco. And the rest featured one of numerous comic book super-heroes—Spiderman, Batman, Superman, and so on. What struck Sandy was that three of the boys had the exact same towel. One of them was her son's.

Sandy went home to her sewing machine that evening. She wanted to create something totally custom, something original. So she began cutting up family bath towels and sewing them back together. After seven gleeful hours of creative bliss, she held up her creation—a far cry from an average beach towel. Instead she had created a vicious dragon-suit towel with wings to wrap around her child, a tail with spikes, and a built-in hood complete with fangs and scary eyes to dry her son's head.

Her son loved it. All the mothers at swimming lessons loved it. Soon Sandy was taking orders to make duckling, frog, unicorn, and wizard wraps.

The additional income was great, but Sandy wanted to some-how turn her once hobby into a real business.

Should she quit her day job?

Will there be enough sales for her business in the future? How can she attract enough clients and let people know about her products? How should she expand her business?

GET COZY WITH YOUR DAY JOB

All too often we hear about owners of new boutique businesses who dive in before testing the water and establishing a solid foundation. When you dive in, you don't really know how viable your business will be, because you haven't tested your concept well enough. Are you currently making money? Are you getting referrals? These two aspects of business are extremely important considerations before you hold your breath, leap off the edge, and turn in that resignation. Use the money from your day job to skyrocket your progress by investing in professional branding help as well as top-notch marketing and branding materials. Hold off on quitting your day job until you have given your business a strong foundation.

Money is obvious. You need to know that your product is priced for profit and will actually sell. Referrals might not be so obvious. You might think they are something you can wait for until *you're in business for real*. But you can't wait for them. Are people diggin' what you do? Are they already telling their friends about you, or are their friends asking about you? If they are, you're in a great position. However, if you're stumped—if you can't remember the last time someone referred a friend to you—then you need to step back and find some answers before you make the leap. For now, stick with your day job. If you have yet to truly open the doors of your business, are considering a new endeavor, or are already acting as a business owner even though you still have a day job, we suggest getting cozy with your cubicle until you consider the following:

1. Your Customers: You don't have a business without customers, and just because you open a shop doesn't mean they'll show up. Consider the story of the former television news photographer who moved from Ohio to Chicago to open a video production facility. He also bought everything. Set up a studio. Then he realized that he didn't know anyone in town. He had no connections. He had no clients. The point is, get customers before you get out of your day job. If you're a stay-at-home parent, grow before you build an office or studio or before you rent a place. If you want to open a restaurant, get some catering business before you open your first location. Once you get some business, monitor your progress. Just because you have one or two clients doesn't mean you'll have enough income to support yourself without a steady paycheck.

2. Your Cash Flow: Yes, you can operate a small business on a small budget, but keep in mind that in order for you to walk away from your day job, your business needs to be able to fund itself (operating expenses, marketing expenses, equipment, etc.) *and* your personal needs (food, clothing, health insurance, shelter, Pinot Grigio, etc.). We see too many people assume that they can quit their day job as soon as they sell their first gadget and go with the "build it and they will come" strategy. That really is a field of dreams, and more often than not, your business will fail before it gets off the ground. Consider Theresa, a custom-jewelry designer from Ohio. She quit her job as a dental hygienist because she attended an arts festival that generated a ton of business. For the first two months, Theresa worked day and night to fill orders, and she made a lot of money. But she also didn't have time to continue marketing. Soon, the flurry of customers was gone—and so was her profit. And guess what? Theresa couldn't afford to buy booth space at the next fair, and she couldn't afford her next month's rent. She ended up making it one more month by maxing out her credit. Then every sale she was making was simply floating her credit. Eventually, she ended up moving in with her mother. It was a bad deal all around.

3. Your Timeline: Growing a business takes time—especially a boutique business where you're building long-term relationships with your customers. Figure out how much money the business requires to pay its monthly bills. Figure out how much money you need to survive. And try to figure out how long it will take you to get to that point if you grow your business while working at your day job. Pay special attention to things that could impact your schedule—billing cycles, seasonal trends, etc. Consider Jeremy, a software developer from South Carolina. He quit his day job as a programmer at a financial institution to build software that he could rebrand and customize for numerous clients. He got his first contract and started programming. And that's when he realized he wouldn't get paid until delivery—nearly four months after his last paycheck.

4. Your Brand: Okay, it's tempting to think that you could quit your day job if you just took on some extra work that didn't fit inside your brand. But it's important to measure the impact that outside-the-brand work might create. A boutique personal trainer might be tempted to teach a few spin classes at the big-box gym. But what happens to that trainer's elite price tag when she's now available to the masses for a lower rate? Yes, there are ways to create cash flow without letting your current customers know, but how is that different from keeping your day job? It's worth it to consider keeping your job until you absolutely have to let it go.

5. Your Attitude: Before you quit your day job, give yourself an attitude check. Do you want to quit because you hate your job and your boss's breath stinks like stale coffee? Or is your business your passion? Is it the thing that captures your every thought? Ask any boutique business owner why they're successful and one of the answers they're all sure to give is "Because I love it." But, there's more. You also have to love the business portion of being in business. You have to love being responsible for all the details, even if you eventually have the luxury to delegate the invoices, the sales calls, the marketing, the customer relationships, and, yes, taxes. Okay, so you don't have to *love* all those things, but you can't hate the responsibility for them either. The perks of working for yourself are fantastic. You make the rules. You live your passion. The money can be phenomenal. The freedom to take vacations, set your pay, and meet great people is priceless. With freedom comes responsibility. It can mean long, late hours. It can mean working while you're on vacation because you are the only one who knows the answers. It could mean you're delivering a client order at 10:30 p.m. on Christmas Eve. It can mean constant attention and focus. There are a lot of sacrifices that accompany the benefits. Do you have the right attitude to handle those sacrifices?

If you've taken a long hard look at each of these five points and feel that you're ready to take the leap, congratulations! We just want you to think carefully before you ditch that drag of a day job and run off into the entrepreneurial jungle. Remember, being a boutique business means that you have the luxury of starting small. Once you're consistently pleasing a small group of committed customers and offering products and services in a way that can't be imitated, you're ready to grow your business sustainably and prepare for taking it on full time. Good luck!

> "You have to love the business portion of being in business. You have to love being responsible for all the details."

ACKNOWLEDGMENTS

WE APPRECIATE ALL OF THE help so many wise and generous people have provided to us throughout this long, evolving process.

For the clients of Sarah Petty Photography, you have our gratitude for your years of unwavering support and for enabling Sarah to create a business where she can give the time and attention necessary to create heirloom artwork for your homes.

The Joy of Marketing has tens of thousands of clients who have contributed to our thinking over the years. Without you, we'd have no one with which to share our ideas, strategies, and inspiration. We are blessed with an incredibly active, caring, and engaged community and without you, it would have been difficult to write this book.

During the writing of this book, we talked with small business owners in many different industries who practice the boutique business model day in and day out. We've mentioned them in the book and are grateful to them for openly sharing their stories. We wish you all continued success.

Andy Brinson, Rebecca Brooks, Lora Carr, Andria Crawford-Whitehead, Dr. William Cron, Myra Hoffman, Jill Liebhaber, Todd Nordstrom, and Jennifer Pearson weighed in on the book in its infancy and provided invaluable feedback on the direction of the book. We are forever thankful for your insightfulness and for being unafraid to share the good and the bad.

We have utmost respect and appreciation for our team at Greenleaf Book Group including Kris Pauls, Aaron Hierholzer, Natalie Navar, and Kim Lance. Thank you for guiding us through the dark places, the nooks and crannies, and the twisty roads to getting this book out of us in its best possible form. You're the best in the business and worth every penny.

Finally, we are thankful to the teams at Sarah Petty Photography, The Joy of Marketing, and our amazing and supportive families for your patience with us while we had to put many other things aside when on deadline for the book. You bring so much joy to our lives and we're lucky to have all of you.

the *joy* of marketing™

We hope you learned a lot by reading our book. Now you know how to build a business that is Worth Every Penny. But you may need ideas on how to market that business to attract the right clients.

As the authors of this book, we'd like to invite you to enjoy a free trial membership of Café Joy, our hands-on monthly program geared toward marketing a boutique business.

If you desire more specialized marketing support, this program will help you build your brand by focusing on beautiful promotional pieces that encourage client interaction while also paying attention to the important details in your business.

Sign up for your free trial membership at
www.thejoyofmarketing.com/wortheverypennycafejoy

ADDITIONAL RESOURCES

The Joy of Marketing
www.thejoyofmarketing.com
The main site where you can learn more about our
company and our products.

Worth Every Penny
www.wortheverypennybook.com
The official book site.

Joy Blog
www.thejoyofmarketing.com/blog
Our company blog about small business marketing ideas.

Joy Resources
www.thejoyofmarketing.com/free
Strategies, audio education, white papers, newsletters
and more ... all free.

Joy Products
www.thejoyofmarketing.com/shop
www.cafejoy.com
Audio and video education, plus dynamic marketing
templates to differentiate your small business.

Joy Speaking
To have Sarah Petty speak to your group or company
contact us at: speaking@thejoyofmarketing.com

Joy Facebook
www.facebook.com/thejoyofmarketing
Catch up on what's new at The Joy of Marketing.

Joy Twitter
www.twitter.com/sarahpetty
www.twitter.com/erinverbeck
Follow Sarah and Erin's daily adventures.

Joy Video
www.youtube.com/thejoyofmarketing
Our presentations and teachings on video.

Stuff We Like
www.thejoyofmarketing.com/sarahsfavorites
A list of books, sites and other things we enjoy.

Email
info@thejoyofmarketing.com